Content

THE
PROCESSING PINNACLE

An Educator's Guide to Better Processing

I WK

Steven Simpson ■ Dan Miller ■ Buzz Bocher

Am B

Published by:

Wood 'N' Barnes Publishing
2717 NW 50th, Oklahoma City, OK 73112
(405) 942-6812

Cover Art by Blue Designs
Copyediting & Layout Design by Ramona Cunningham

Printed in the United States of America
Oklahoma City, Oklahoma
ISBN # 1-885473-63-X

to

Manyu and Clare

Darci and Avalon

Pat and Sean

Preface

In the world of experiential education, the first decade of the 21st century may come to be remembered as the decade of processing. Processing or the debriefing of experience has been part of education ever since there has been an education profession—isn't the Socratic method, after all, actually a form of processing?—but the experiential education profession has recently embraced processing in a way that was not obvious before. Not long ago, most experiential education conferences had only a couple of sessions dedicated to processing. Today processing is a major subtheme of these conferences, and almost every time block during an experiential education conference will have a processing workshop. One or two new books on processing are published every year. One or two books a year may not seem like a lot, but only 10 years ago an experiential educator's entire library might contain only one or two books. Clifford Knapp's *Lasting Lessons* and Nadler and Luckner's *Processing the Adventure Experience* come to mind.[1] Most important, processing has been elevated in the minds of many experiential educators from a skill that can be learned after other aspects of facilitation have been mastered to a skill that is an integral part of even basic experiential education training.

So here is *The Processing Pinnacle: An Educator's Guide to Better Processing*. The obvious question is, "What does this book have that makes it different from other processing books?" *The Processing Pinnacle* is a book of practical theory; as experiential educators develop their repertoires of processing techniques, *The Processing Pinnacle* offers a systematic, four-stage approach for using those techniques in a way that best serves students. The book introduces a few new processing techniques, but it is not a cookbook of activities. Instead the book is intended to help educators apply more effectively the processing techniques that they already use.

The Processing Pinnacle also offers encouragement to experiential educators who are uncertain of their ability to facilitate group processing. All of the information in this book has been presented in more than a dozen experiential education workshops in North America and Asia, and participants commonly made comments like, "I've been processing for a couple years, but was never sure whether I was doing it right. I still have much to learn, but at least I now feel like I am on a good path."

And "a good path" is an appropriate way to make this point. *The Processing Pinnacle* is one of several ways to look at processing. As McKinley, a reoccurring character in the book, puts it, "Processing is an intuitive practice, and the Processing Pinnacle is an attempt to put logic and structure to something that is not particularly logical." We hope such an approach will help readers become better facilitators in the art of reflective learning.

Introduction

The introductory section of *The Processing Pinnacle* is a three-part overview of experiential education processing. Chapter 1 is a conversation between Yangtze and McKinley, two experiential educators with opposing views on the role of processing. Its purpose is to present some of the issues that the book addresses. Chapter 2 defines processing as it will be used in *The Processing Pinnacle*. Many readers will find this chapter fairly basic, but even seasoned experiential educators might be interested in the chapter's list of the primary purposes for processing. Chapter 3 lists the difficulties of processing. It includes an anecdotal summary of a processing workshop where we asked professional experiential educators why they think processing is a hard skill to master.

SECTION ONE

A Conversation on Reflection

Processing is like a campfire. After struggling to get the thing started, you can either stoke the inferno until the heat pushes people away or carefully tend the fire and let people lose themselves in the flickering flames.

We would like to start this book with a conversation between two people sitting at a campfire. The conversation is a reflection. It is, to some extent, a reflection on reflection, because the purpose of the story is to point out the complexities of processing. The people in the story represent two distinct approaches to processing or debriefing an experience. As you read the story, identify the perspective that is most like your own.

McKinley gingerly fed two pieces of dried birch into the campfire. Stoking the fire broke the silence of the secluded campsite, but it also, in a few minutes, would cut the chill that had set in since the sun had dropped below the pines. He looked back at the tent where Yangtze was rummaging through her pack for a sweater.

"Sure you don't want hot water for tea?" he asked.

"No thanks," she said. "I just want to hear about your day, then climb into bed. I'll be right there."

For four straight summers McKinley and Yangtze had vacationed together in the north woods. Their definition of being on vacation together, however, generally meant doing things separately. The two had met several years back at an experiential education conference and discovered that they wrestled with the same problem when it came to spending time in nature. Both wanted to be alone to experience solitude, but discovered that they got lonely when doing extended trips by themselves. It was Yangtze who suggested that they go on trips together, doing things separately during the day, but sharing a base camp to have someone to talk to at night. The daytime provided solitude; the evening took the edge off being alone. The arrangement worked so well that it became an annual event.

Yangtze pulled her sweater over her head and sat opposite the fire from McKinley.

Yangtze :   Do you know how lucky we are to be sitting around a campfire? Whenever I do it I realize how wonderful it is and I wonder why I don't do it more often. Even when I teach sailing or paddling at the outdoor center, it's usually just day stuff, and I'm back in my apartment by the time it gets dark. There must have been a time when just about every human being in the world ended the evening by staring into a fire and thinking about the day. Now the campfire is a simple pleasure that's lost to most people.

How do you self-reflect?

McKinley: Yeah, I know what you mean. I have a fire sixty, maybe seventy, times a year, but I never take it for granted. Most of them, of course, are with groups on a climbing trip. It's usually after a day of making sure novice climbers are safe, so I come to the fire still a little bit wired. The flames calm me down before bed. I also use the fire as a place to process the day.

Yangtze: You use the campfire for processing? Doesn't that take some of the magic out of it?

McKinley: I don't know. I never thought about it in terms of magic. The fire's often the first time all day when everybody's not busy, so it seems like a good time for me to ask a few questions about what everybody learned. You just said yourself that fire is good for reflection. I just formalize that reflection a bit.

Yangtze: But the reason I like campfires so much is that they aren't formalized. I can talk or not talk, and either is fine. If you make people process, you're making them think and talk about stuff that doesn't come up on its own. You're ruining the spontaneity. Look at the campfires you and I have. I learn things, but that is secondary to relaxing and poking a stick in the coals. I'd be ticked off if you all of sudden started debriefing me.

Is your processing fairly formal? Fairly informal?

McKinley: My campfires on climbing trips usually last hours, and I'm only taking up twenty or thirty minutes for processing. And don't confuse you and me sitting around a fire with other people sitting around a fire. My groups won't reflect without me pushing them to. They talk a lot around the fire, but it's almost never about nature or what they did on the rock. They talk about music or partying or the TV shows they are missing by being out on the trip. They usually come around to concluding that sitting around the fire is better than being back in town, but otherwise they don't reflect. Maybe a few do, but those are late-nighters who stick around the fire after everybody else has gone to bed.

Besides, you and I are here for different reasons than the people in my groups.

We're here to play. They are there to learn something. Education should be fun, but educational outings and recreational outings are two different things.

Are your programs primarily recreation or education? Do you make a distinction?

Yangtze: I don't think they're different. I know that you are bringing people out to nature to work on self-esteem and cooperation and stuff like that, but isn't interaction with nature really the important thing? When I take people on a canoe trip, the overriding goal is simply to get people on the water. They slow down, relax, spend some time in a place that is conducive to reflection. The self-esteem and cooperation stuff are gravy, and those benefits only occur because the natural setting is so unique.

McKinley: No, for me, getting out into nature is not enough. I work mostly with at-risk youth or corporate groups. The people who hire me want clear results. A quiet weekend in the woods isn't going to cut it with the organizers, so a half hour around the fire is a cheap price to pay. If I am very focused in my processing techniques, I can get the processing done in a short time, then let people talk about whatever they want.

What are the expectations of your clients? Specific? Open-ended?

Yangtze: What does "focused in your processing techniques" mean? That you jam a concept down their throats?

McKinley: If you're asking whether I structure processing to bring out specific points, yeah, but I don't think that's jamming anything down anybody's throat. I have goals in my teaching, and the processing is designed to bring out those goals. I might want a group to think about self-esteem, so I ask questions about that. I might want to stress climbing techniques, so I structure the processing around that.

What is more important in your own programing—the pre-determined goals or the unexpected events of the day?

Yangtze: If the campfire conversations that you and I have work for us, why do you have to make the discussions with your groups so formal? As long as you nudge discussion toward the events of the day, what difference does it make how focused it is? When we finish talking, I feel like we've reflected. I tell you why I've had a good day paddling up and down the river, and you do the same about your hike.

McKinley: You and I do get more out of our discussions than I sometimes get from a processing session with my clients, but it's our personalities, not the techniques. You are reflective by nature—and although you probably don't appreciate it, that's unusual. I'm not naturally reflective myself, but have become more so since working with groups. My inclination is to go, go, go, and forget about processing, but that's the climber in me, not the facilitator. I make my clients slow down to process, and I guess some of it has rubbed off. Most people aren't reflective. That's not a criticism. That's just the way it is. My clients will sit around a campfire and talk all night, but it's mostly chatter. Only occasionally is it anything to do with the day.

Are most people naturally reflective? What makes a person reflective?

Yangtze: It seems to me you don't trust the process. I can understand that you are strict when you teach climbing. A mistake might mean someone gets hurt. It's the same when I'm paddling on the river. But do you think that you are carrying your strict methods over to the processing part? You give me too much credit when you say that I am more reflective than other people. I think that if you just plopped them down around a campfire, they'd get the point. They might not talk about the stuff that you want them to talk about, but something good would come out of it.

McKinley: But why not teach people to be more reflective and give them step-by-step lessons on how to process? I'm taking people by the hand when we process, but all the time I'm doing that, they're learning something. It's a progression. Because I force them to process from the very first day, people figure out that processing is as much a part of the program as the action.

What strategies do you use to help participants process on their own?

Yangtze: But are you really sure that your training is what made the difference? Maybe it's time in nature that has encouraged reflection. Maybe they need a little time to get the superficial topics out of the way, and once that is done, their reflective sides emerge. If you put people in front of campfires for three or four nights in a row, they will start thinking about things they haven't thought about before.

McKinley: That's a good point. It's also a pretty good criticism of the rush-'em-in/rush-'em-out programs that you and I do. One or two days isn't enough time for people to clear their heads and start to reflect on their own. But that's exactly why I feel like I have to process so much. Because I don't work with people very long, I can't just assume that the lessons will sink in by themselves.

What is an ideal program length to promote a reflective atmosphere?

Yangtze: I'm not saying that you shouldn't process. I process with most of my programs, but it's less structured than the kind of thing you describe. I would never think to say, "Everybody be at the campfire at 7:00 p.m. We're going to process."

McKinley: But I think that the most successful groups are the ones where I control the processing. Sometimes, I even frontload and tell my groups what it is that they are supposed to learn even before they start anything. I tell the group that the purpose of this day of climbing is to build trust among each other. I tell them up front that each time they go through a belay contract it's like saying "I trust you" and "Your trust is merited." Later that night at the campfire, it is very easy for me to say, "All of you just put your lives in the hands of your coworkers. Why isn't there similar trust back at the workplace?"

Yangtze: Just to be devil's advocate, how do you know that it is trust that the group needs to work on? You don't know those people very well. Maybe they would be better off experiencing a personal relationship with nature, but instead you are deciding that trust is the topic of the day.

When processing, who chooses most of the topics?

McKinley: In a situation where you just let things happen, the people most in tune with experiential education will be fine. It is the folks who need the help who won't know why they're doing what they're doing. They'll have fun climbing, but will have learned nothing about trust or nature or anything else.

Yangtze: I guess I disagree. If the activity and the setting are exceptional, everyone will experience something worthwhile. It's like coming around a bend in a river and startling an eagle. Those things can't be planned. And when they happen, I don't need to gather everyone around to talk about it. Seeing an eagle doesn't need interpretation.

McKinley: I agree, but for me, *that*'s the gravy. I plan for one thing to happen, but am thrilled when something better pops up. If I think it is appropriate, I shift my purpose to the better thing.

Yangtze: But how often does that really happen?

McKinley: I usually stick to a plan because I know that the plan works. It's not as if the questions for my question and answer sessions are written in stone, but I do have certain processing techniques that I use a lot.

How much processing preplanning do you do?

Yangtze: And those techniques probably push people along specific paths. The route is set. The topics are predetermined. The reason that I don't plan my processing beforehand is that I know that if I plan, I have already influenced the direction of the processing.

McKinley: Yeah, but I want to influence the direction of the processing. I have goals I want to achieve. My program is planned and my processing is set up to get at certain things. What's wrong with that? It seems like a perfect way to do it.

Are your processing sessions facilitator-controlled or participant-controlled?

Yangtze: Nothing is wrong with it. Just like I scout a river before I take a group there. But a river changes constantly, so I have to be flexible. That's real life. We don't learn by following a plan step-by-step. We learn by having fluid experiences, then processing when something needs to be processed.

McKinley: I understand everything that you are saying. Still by planning, even over-planning, I avoid the unexpected. I can predict just about everything that is going to happen, and that includes the processing as much as the actual climbing. But that's the way I want it. I might be missing a special teaching moment every once in a while, but I also am avoiding the bad and the boring. If I follow the same routine group after group, I'm the only one who knows it's a routine. For clients, it feels new. For them, it is new. Unless I go into autopilot, the experience for them is fresh and exciting. Even though I've seen the view from the top of a mountain countless times, the people I take to the summit think of it as a new discovery. The same with processing. If I get the same semi-cliché responses during most of my processing sessions, so what? They're cliché to me, but they might be novel ideas for the people in the group.

Yangtze: It feels contrived.

McKinley: It is contrived. Education is contrived. That's one of the differences between experiential education and experiential learning. Experiential learning is the happenstance that you describe. It's gleaning the lessons of life when you bump into them. Experiential education is more formal than that. It's not the same thing as everyday life. It is a contrived experience jammed into a specific place and time. I set objectives, plan an activity, then plan a processing technique that addresses the objectives. Then another objective, another planned activity, and another planned processing technique. I take two or three days to create a series of experiences where people think that they are discovering things on their own—even though the opportunities for discovery were planned well in advance.

What in education is contrived?

Yangtze: You make it sound like I dislike all structure. That's not true. I have structure in my programs, but not nearly the structure that you seem to have in your processing. First you frontload, so everyone knows up front what it is they are supposed to learn. Then you conduct carefully planned question and answer sessions, discussing the same subjects that you covered in the frontloading. You aren't giving people enough credit. You assume they can't process even before you start working with them.

McKinley: You just described my position better than I could have. The people who I work with are generally pretty smart, but nothing about them suggests that they can process on their own. You seem to think that people instinctively have revelations about their experiences. I don't think they do.

Yangtze: Do you know why we spend our days apart from each other?

McKinley: Sure, we both want time alone.

Yangtze: That's only part of it. We also want different things. You want a clear goal. I don't. For me, it's wandering. Whatever happens happens. For you it's a quest with a very specific destination. Yesterday you climbed to the top of Timm's Hill. Today you climbed St. Peter's Dome. For me, I toss my kayak into a river that catches my fancy, and the only thing I know for sure is that I somehow have to get back to my car by the end of the day. I might paddle all day, but I might just as likely fish or go swimming or beach the boat and go for a hike. I think our approaches to processing are different for the same reason. You have something specific that you want every student to learn. I don't care. I create an opportunity and leave it up to each student to learn whatever it is he or she is supposed to learn.

Do your programs address a specific set of goals and objectives? Do they create an atmosphere for spontaneous and unexpected events?

McKinley: That's it. Predetermined outcomes versus whatever happens, happens. In terms of educational philosophy, I'm mainstream, and you're way out there. You think anything experiential is valid just because it is experiential. You also think that anything done outdoors is better than most stuff done indoors, so just getting people outside is worthwhile. To me, that is too much left to chance. Predetermined outcomes, assessment procedures, and all of the other formalities that you don't like give experiential education structure. It's your "anything goes" attitude that bugs traditional educators, and I don't blame them.

Yangtze: I know that you don't think I'm a flake, but that's how you make me sound—like someone who puts flowers in her hair and dances in the moonlight....

McKinley: I bet you've done that.

Yangtze: Okay, bad example. The point I want to make is that my faith in the teaching power of nature is not New Age mumbo-jumbo. I've thought about this stuff, and I've worked in structured programs before—I think programs are better when they are open-ended. I have a grab bag of processing techniques ready, but I use them only when the moment presents itself. If I don't use them at all, that's okay, too. People will still learn something, and it probably won't be something that I dictated that they learn.

McKinley: I've thought about all this, too, but have come to the opposite conclusion. I want to determine what students learn. I know this means some students think I am too rigid. I can see it when participants roll their eyes as if to say, "Oh God, he's going to make us process again," but I don't care. They roll their eyes when I check their climbing knot for the tenth time too, but seeing me check and double check knots makes them better climbers. I don't see the downside of making lessons explicit.

Yangtze: The downside is that it's your lesson, not the students'. Still as much as I would never do things the way that you do them, I am glad that someone is. Between us, we cover a lot of ground and reach a lot of people.

McKinley: You're right. I'll teach the regular people, and you can rein in the kooks.

Yangtze: Oh, I don't want to rein them in! It's the regular people, not the kooks, that I need to work on. They need to loosen up.

McKinley: So you do have goals to your program! You want to undo all the structure that traditional education worked so hard to create.

Does your educational philosophy promote structure? Does it discourage structure?

Yangtze: Maybe that is what I want. I want people to sense freedom, so I try to turn them loose.

McKinley: Are you sure they're ready for that freedom? My perspective is that I have to teach people something before I turn them loose. Yours is that they've been over-taught and overtrained already, so you turn them loose right off the bat.

Yangtze: You're right! That is the difference between us! You think that people need to be taught how to reflect, so you teach them. I think people already know how to reflect, but that traditional education has buried this natural ability under a big stack of rules and... and... and other stuff. If I can get people away from classrooms and lectures and tests, they will reflect on their own.

Why do you process?

McKinley: So who's right?

Yangtze: Well, ten minutes ago I was sure it was me. Now I'm not as sure. The important question is which approach makes people more reflective in their daily lives, and I honestly don't know the answer.

McKinley: That is the question, isn't it? It's not so much that people reflect after a specific activity, but that they become more reflective in general, more reflective in their lives.

Yangtze: Yeah. (pause) Another question is whether I have some tea now or just go to bed.

McKinley: That one's easy. Let me start up the stove and heat some water.

What Is Processing?

*Processing is like broccoli. Sometimes thought of as only a
side dish, it usually is the most healthy part of the meal.
Serve it too often, however, and people say,
"Oh no! Not broccoli again!"*

Most educators who pick up this book already know what processing is. Classroom teachers, interpretative naturalists, adventure programmers, ropes course facilitators, camp counselors,
and other experiential educators do not read about processing
to find out what it is; they read about it to become better processors. Still it seems that a short definition of processing is an appropriate introduction to the book. This introduction has three
parts. The first defines processing, the second states several
reasons that experiential educators process, and the third, with
the use of a brief story, summarizes what may be the prevalent
attitude toward the art of processing.

What is Processing?

At its most basic, experiential education programs have two overall components. One is the action, and the other is the reflection.
Another term for the reflection is processing. Luckner and Nadler
define it as "an activity that is structured to encourage individuals to plan, reflect, describe, analyze, and communicate about experiences."[1] Sugerman, Doherty, Garvey, and Gass say about the
same thing by defining processing as "a cognitive activity where
people recapture their experience, think about it, mull it over,
and evaluate it."[2] Both of these definitions capture the key point
that processing is a facilitator's decision not to leave reflection to
chance. As Joplin puts it, processing makes sure that the action
components of an experience do not go unquestioned, unreal-

ized, unintegrated, or unorganized.[3]   In other words, processing is a planned activity designed to give meaning to the action.

According to Chinese Tao thinking, action and reflection cannot exist without each other. The action, or yang component, of an experience connotes movement leading to change. Something exciting occurs, and the energy of this excitement moves people in new directions. Conversely the reflection, or yin component, of an experience connotes meaning.[4] Reflection organizes and interprets the action so that any change that occurs is understood and appreciated. Without reflection, the positive aspects of the action are either fleeting or out of control. Without action, reflection is intellectual posturing without real-world implications.

Clifford Knapp, in his book *Lasting Lessons*, points out that the word processing has a number of synonyms, terms such as debriefing, critiquing, closure, elaboration, bridging, reviewing, and analyzing.[5] In experiential education jargon, however, debriefing and reviewing are the two terms other than processing to show up on a regular basis. Sometimes, debriefing is used as an exact synonym for processing. At other times, it is used as a subcategory of processing, referring only to the processing that occurs *after* the action component. This is in contrast to processing that might occur before or during the action. Processing, debriefing, reviewing—all are equally descriptive terms for reflective practice. This book generally sticks with the word processing, but only for the sake of consistency.

Why Process?

The most common reason for processing is to make clear to all participants the lessons of a specific activity. Some lessons are self-evident to 80% of the participants, and processing reveals those lessons to the 20% who did not discern them on their own. Other lessons of an action are subtle, and just about all of the participants need a processing session to appreciate the implications. In these instances, processing brings to light the less obvious lessons of an experience.

There are many other valid reasons for processing. Some of the primary reasons to process include:

- Making sure *all* participants understand the lessons of the action component of the experience.

- Teaching participants about the importance of reflection and teaching them how to process.

- Allowing participants to express both their positive and negative feelings.

- Helping participants to clarify their thoughts by putting those thoughts into words.

- Analyzing the action. This means breaking down an activity into its component parts to better understand why things happened as they did.

- Synthesizing the action. This means trying to take the events of a specific activity and put them in a broader context; i.e., putting the component parts back together following the analysis.

- Helping give the experience permanence. Obviously, some experiences are so dramatic that they will never be forgotten. For other experiences, processing can help to cement the experience in participants' minds.

- Transferring the lessons of the immediate experience to everyday life.

- Evaluating the experience as to whether it accomplished the stated goals and objectives.

- Promoting the value of experiencing and encouraging participants to fill their lives with a continuous series of educational experiences.

- Bringing closure to an activity.[6]

How Do Educators Feel About Processing?

Some experiential educators think that processing is far and away the most interesting part of their jobs. Others think that processing is more work than it is worth and, as often as not, disrupts the flow of the action. Most educators fall somewhere in between these two extremes. The following real-life scenario might do a good job of generalizing facilitator attitudes toward the complexity of processing:

> At the end of a college course about experiential education methodology, the last day of the class was set aside for reflecting on the semester. One of the processing techniques used on this final day was a human continuum. The instructor drew a 25-foot line on the floor of the classroom and told the students that he would make a series of statements about experiential education. After each statement, the students had to physically move themselves to a point along the line that represented their opinion about the statement. If, for example, a student had extreme feelings about a statement, he would move toward a far end of the line to express that strong opinion. If a student was neutral about the statement or had a centrist opinion, he would express that middle-of-the-road stance by shifting to a spot near the center point of the line. Students were to choose their place independently of where other students lined up, but once all of the students had picked their places on the continuum, everyone was encouraged to look where they positioned themselves in comparison to everyone else.

> "Okay," the leader began, "statement number one. As a participant in this course, I preferred the action parts of the course over the processing parts. If you preferred the action, move to the far right. If you preferred the processing, move to the far left. If you liked the two equally, move to the center." All the students moved to the right half of the continuum. No student was left of center; not one student out of 27 preferred processing over action.

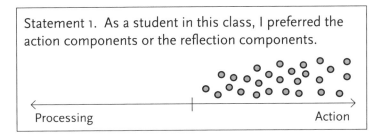

Statement 1. As a student in this class, I preferred the action components or the reflection components.

Processing → Action

Then the leader said, "Okay, statement number two. For this one, I want you to think of yourself as a leader, not as a student. When I facilitate an experience, I prefer facilitating the processing component of an experience to facilitating the action component. If you like processing better, go left. If you like the action, go right. If you like both equally, move to the center." All of the students shuffled right until they were bunched together into the far right quartile. Three quarters of the continuum was completely empty. Every student preferred leading action to leading reflection, and they preferred it by a sizable margin.

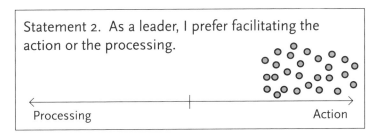

Statement 2. As a leader, I prefer facilitating the action or the processing.

Processing → Action

Then the leader said, "Statement number three. As a student in this class, I learned more from the action parts of the experiences than I did from the processing parts. If you learned more from the action, go right. If you learned more from the processing, go left." Almost en masse, the cluster of students shifted about four steps to the left. They remained to the action half of the continuum, but now were huddled up in the third quartile rather than in the fourth. One student, however, broke off from the rest of the class and moved well into the processing side of the continuum. When the other students all looked at her, she explained, "I'd done most of the group initiatives before, so I didn't learn much during the activity part. But all of the processing stuff was new to me. And quit gawking. I can stand wherever I want."

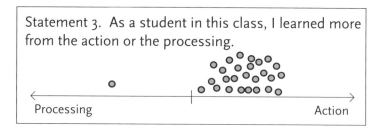

Statement 3. As a student in this class, I learned more from the action or the processing.

Processing   Action

Finally the leader said, "Statement number four. Processing is more important than action. If you think that action is more important than processing, go right. If processing is more important than action, go left." The students broke out of their tight ball and spread out across the continuum. Even after the shift, slightly more than half of the students remained right of center, but for the first time, several of the students preferred processing to action.

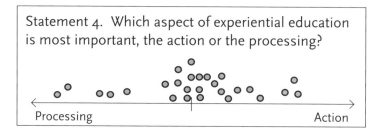

Statement 4. Which aspect of experiential education is most important, the action or the processing?

Processing   Action

After the fourth statement, the instructor ended the human continuum and asked everyone to sit in a circle to talk about the results of the technique. Out of the discussion, it became evident that one of the main things learned during the semester was the importance of processing. In fact, some students felt that the instructor had gone overboard in presenting the attributes of processing. Prior to taking the course, most students had not processed at all in their own leadership. Now they would. They had, over the course of the semester, compiled a repertoire of processing techniques, and they planned to use some of them.

Still the students enjoyed the action component of experiential education more than they did the processing. And although they now felt comfortable facilitating some of the processing techniques learned in class, they were unsure whether their processing sessions would be of much value. Students felt that they had some of the mechanics of processing, but not the art of it. And finally, in spite of the course's emphasis on processing, the students still believed that the action component was more important than the processing. They felt that the true value of experiential education resided in the action, not the facilitated reflection. Sometimes the lessons of an action presented themselves without much reflection. Other times the people involved in the action reflected on their own and gleaned the lessons without a processing session. In other words, action could sometimes stand on its own, whereas reflection without action was not, in the opinions of the students, even experiential education.

Obviously this anecdote expresses the opinions of a non-random sample of novice experiential educators, but it might be an accurate representation of experiential educators in general. Processing is seen as important, but also as more difficult to facilitate than the action. Sometimes processing feels like a secondary component to the main attraction. It is the broccoli of experiential education—vital to a well-balanced program, but except to those who are very process-oriented, not as interesting as the main course.

To carry the broccoli metaphor just a little further, processing is an acquired taste. In fact, the overriding purpose of this book is to make processing more palatable to those who are tempted to push it under the plate. It is to make a convincing statement as to the importance of processing and, at the same time, to suggest ways for making processing easier for the facilitator and more engaging for the participants.

Ten Reasons Why Processing Is Difficult

> A grab bag of processing techniques is like the rules
> of good grammar. Grammar can tell you how to write a
> letter. It can't tell you when to write, nor what to say.*

Nearly all experiential educators want to improve their process-ing skills. This applies to seasoned educators just as much as it does to novice facilitators. In comparison to other facilita-tion skills such as introducing a group initiative, belaying a high element on a ropes course, or leading a nature hike, processing is the one component of facilitation that never feels quite good enough. Whereas some aspects of experiential education even-tually become second nature, processing remains a challenge.

Processing is difficult. It is as simple as that. In fact, it is a truism within experiential education that processing is the most difficult part of the facilitator's workload. It is not enough, however, to simply acknowledge that processing is hard. To stop there would be the equivalent of observing that a group of people failed to work together during a team-building initiative, but never asking the group why the teamwork was not there. Asking the question can be the big first step to confronting the overall problem. With that in mind, the purpose of this chapter is to answer the question, "Why is processing difficult?"

Below are 10 reasons why processing is likely the most difficult part of the experiential education profession. Some of the rea-

---

* This statement is a misquote of the stoic philosopher Epictetus. The real quote is "...when you must write something to your friend, grammar will tell you what words you must write; but whether you should write or not, grammar will not tell you." In *The Discourses of Epictetus*, Book 1, Chapter 1.

sons are obvious, some not. Taken as a whole, it is an imposing list. No wonder processing is hard.

1. LEADING A PROCESSING SESSION IS INTIMIDATING.

   Perhaps the overriding reason that processing is difficult is that it can be an intimidating responsibility—to the point that new facilitators avoid it and are slow to develop their processing skills. Certainly it is one of the things that even gung ho assistant leaders often are willing to leave to their senior colleagues. The only way to get good at processing is to lead processing sessions, but learning by trial and error is very much like public speaking, and it scares people. Pearson and Smith point out that the transition from the action component of an experience to the processing component changes the role of the facilitator from an omniscient observer to a mere member of the group. When experiential educators facilitate the action, they usually remain a peripheral presence with all of the authority and all of the knowledge. As soon as they sit down with the group to lead a question and answer session, they become much more a part of the group. They forfeit total control. The distance between facilitator and participant shrinks, and the facilitator is exposed to questioning, to uncontrolled emotions, and to divergent and sometimes irrelevant ideas.[1]

   Part of effective processing is practice. It is facilitators moving outside their own comfort zones and developing their processing skills through frequent practice. Honing processing skills on the job is one place where co-facilitation is especially useful; junior staff can take the lead during a processing session, but know that a senior facilitator is always there to back them up.

2. NO TWO PROCESSING SESSIONS ARE EXACTLY THE SAME.

   One of the most obvious reasons that processing is hard is because each group of participants has its own personality, so no processing session is routine. Even when facilitators have the specifics of a processing session planned out ahead of time, part of effective processing is the ability to deviate from a plan whenever necessary. A facilitator must then come up with the right question or the right processing technique at a moment's notice. This is, in fact, the Socratic method. Socrates, perhaps the greatest teacher in the history of the Western world, might have been skilled at drawing insightful statements out of his students by coming up with the right sequence of questions at just the right moment, but the rest of us struggle with this task.

Part of effective processing is the ability to deviate from a plan. An important skill of a competent processor is the Socratic method, the ability to come up with good questions at just the right time.

3. FACILITATORS MAY NOT PREPARE ADEQUATELY FOR THEIR PROCESSING SESSIONS.

Because processing often is very effective when done in an impromptu manner, some experienced educators trust their intuitive processing skills to the point that they don't plan their processing sessions. Instead of having a plan that might be abandoned if the action component takes an unexpected turn, they do not bother to plan their processing at all and rely entirely on their ability to think on their feet. Armed with a grab bag of processing tools and a mental list of generic processing questions, these facilitators trust that the appropriate processing method will present itself when it is time to process. Even though the textbook approach to experiential education is to determine the processing method in advance of delivering the program, they simply identify the place in the program where processing will most likely occur and then wing it. These same facilitators set goals, they choose specific activities, they carefully prepare the setting, but then do not pre-plan the processing sessions. The action component of an experience is orchestrated, but the processing component is expected to materialize on its own.

Part of effective processing is having a processing plan. Competent processors are flexible as to the direction their processing might take, but not to the point of abandoning all planning.

4. THE PURPOSES FOR PROCESSING ARE NUMEROUS, MAYBE TOO NUMEROUS TO KEEP STRAIGHT.

There are many valid reasons for processing (see chapter 2 of this book for a list). Sometimes processing sessions have a scattered and incoherent feel to them because facilitators try to accomplish too much in a limited period of time. For example, they want to make sure that the goals of the activity are understood, but they also want to make sure that all of the participants get to express their feelings; additionally they want to generate a memorable metaphor that can be used when the processing session shifts to applications for everyday life—and all of this must get accomplished in 15 minutes. Good processing should focus on and try to accomplish only one or two things at a time.

Part of effective processing is not trying to accomplish all things in every processing session. One reason for planning the processing session is to explicitly identify the specific objectives of that specific processing session.

5. FACILITATOR TRAINING SOMETIMES SLIGHTS PROCESSING.

One fundamental reason that facilitators find processing difficult is that they may not have been adequately trained in it. Most training sessions for new experiential educators emphasize the technical aspects of the job. They cover the nuts and bolts of an agency's programing. On a ropes course, for example, training sessions generally include belay techniques and the instructions for setting up group initiatives. With a wilderness adventure program, training includes a countless number of things, but seldom techniques for leading an insightful conversation around the campfire. Very few experiential educators would say that the reflection component is less important than the action component, but in terms of basic training, matters of content and physical safety take precedence over processing skills.

Part of effective processing is having been trained in processing. If it does not occur during a facilitator's initial training, it needs to occur on the job, at continuing education workshops, at conferences, and during subsequent trainings.

6. PEOPLE ARE NOT NATURALLY REFLECTIVE.

Christian theologian Thomas Merton said that people—at least Americans—are not reflective.[2] They are extremely action-oriented and tend to live lives where reflection is not an everyday occurrence. When presented with a challenge that requires action, these people jump right in and do an excellent job. When asked to reflect on that action, however, they do not know what to do. Many people have not been taught to reflect, nor is reflection part of their nature. Therefore, when an experiential educator establishes a learning pattern of both action and reflection, the action comes easily to the participants; the reflection does not.

Part of effective processing is teaching participants 1) the importance of reflection and 2) techniques for reflection.

7. NOT EVERYTHING MERITS REFLECTION.

Facilitators sometimes make participants process even when the action component has generated nothing worthy of reflection. Quality education is a combination of action and reflection, but this does not mean that good facilitation is an inflexible format of action followed by reflection followed by action followed by reflection. Experiential education often takes people outside their comfort zones, and new surroundings and new challenges usually deserve reflection, but this is not a hard and fast rule. Processing for the sake of processing, or processing just because it has been a while since a group has processed, can be like trying to draw water from a dry well.

Part of effective processing is knowing more than how to process; it is also knowing when to and when not to process.

8. THE BAR IS SET UNREASONABLY HIGH.

In the action phase of experiential education, the participants are allowed, even encouraged, to fail. Occasional failure shows that the participants are challenging themselves. Failure also provides fodder for an interesting processing session. Processing sessions, however, are not given the same latitude as the action components when it comes to sub-par performance. A lousy processing session often is interpreted as something gone wrong. Maybe the facilitator lacked the skills to lead the session. Maybe the participants did not take the experience seriously. They were up for the fun and games, but refused to get serious during the processing session.

Is this perspective really fair? If processing is so difficult, shouldn't people be allowed to have lousy processing sessions without concluding that something went wrong? It is, after all, as much a learning experience as the action.

Part of effective processing is having realistic expectations of what processing can accomplish. It is accepting that not every processing session is going to be stimulating and insightful.

9. THE POSITIVE RESULTS OF PROCESSING MAY NOT BE APPARENT.

A processing session may be much more effective than it seemed at the time. In other words, some of the benefits of processing do not show themselves during the actual processing session. Some participants may reflect, but not speak up. Other participants may not have profound thoughts at the time, but the processing session may open the door for valuable reflection later.

Still others may like to express their feelings, but because it is difficult to put those feelings into words, they choose not to speak. There is no excuse for a weakly led processing session, but a processing session done well may be working much better than a facilitator realizes. When an action component goes well, it is obvious, and the participants break into spontaneous applause. When processing goes well, it is possible that no one fully understands what has been accomplished.

Part of effective processing is having faith in the process of experiential education.

10. THERE ARE MORE THAN TEN REASONS WHY PROCESSING IS DIFFICULT.

No doubt many educators reading this list of ten reasons have concluded, "This list is okay, but it doesn't even include the reasons why I find processing difficult. What about the difficulty of finding effective metaphors? What about the times when processing touches on personal issues that require the skills of a trained counselor? What about...?" The primary reason that processing is difficult is that many factors contribute to the difficulty. At a recent Association for Experiential Education workshop on processing, session participants were asked straight out why processing was hard.[3] Their long list of responses included the following:

- Constant question and answer gets boring.
- The facilitator doesn't want to let go of his agenda.
- It's difficult to listen to participants and simultaneously formulate your next question.
- Participants have trouble finding a metaphor without the facilitator giving it to them.
- Facilitating the timing between action and reflection is confusing.
- Participants don't want to process.
- It's hard to keep participants focused on the subject at hand.

- When working with a group for an extended period of time, it's difficult to keep processing fresh and original.

- Responding to unexpected, but valid comments by participants is challenging.

- Groups often are too large for effective processing.

- Processing is a new model/new language for participants.

- Participants are understandably reluctant to share feelings.

- Participants do not buy into the value of processing.

- Participants do not transition well from action to inaction.

- Facilitators do not have the skills to process well.

- Emotional safety issues are intimidating for both facilitators and participants.

Part of effective processing is each facilitator identifying his or her personal stumbling blocks when it comes to processing, then addressing them.

This top ten list was not generated merely to highlight the difficulty of becoming a competent processor. The list is an analysis of the task, breaking down the imposing whole into its component parts. Experiential education tends to be holistic, looking at the big picture rather than the little pieces. Here is a case, however, where looking at the individual pieces sheds light on the whole. It gives experiential educators a handle or two for addressing the challenges of becoming a better processor. If the overall task of quality processing is overwhelming, then incremental improvement by addressing specific sub-challenges may be the best approach.

A Processing Quiz

Section Two presents a quiz designed to help experiential educators clarify their processing tendencies. The first chapter in this section (chapter 4) is a quiz that we invite readers to take. The quiz consists of 12 fairly long multiple-choice questions. It takes up to 30 minutes to complete. In workshops, we have used both a long form and a short form of the quiz. The short quiz has been criticized as not containing enough information. The long quiz has been criticized as being too time consuming. For the book, we include only the long form. We suggest that readers find a time when they can give the quiz a half hour of undisturbed time, read each question carefully, and answer how they would handle each of the 12 situations. The conclusion of chapter 4 shows how to score the quiz.

The second chapter (chapter 5) consists of two parts. The first part is an explanation of a processing continuum and processing matrix. The second part uses the matrix to interpret the quiz results. If a person chooses not to take the quiz, it is still important to read the first part of chapter 5, as the continuum and the matrix are a lead-in to the Processing Pinnacle and the chapters that follow.

SECTION TWO

A Processing Quiz

Processing is like a multiple-choice test. The students often spend too much time trying to figure out which answer the teacher is looking for.

Two chapters from now this book will finally get around to defining the Processing Pinnacle, the concept for which the book is named. Before reading about the Pinnacle, however, we invite you to take a short multiple-choice quiz about processing. If you take the quiz, take it before reading any of the chapters that follow, as those chapters may influence the way you answer. The quiz is intended to be fun. It certainly will serve as a lead-in to the rest of the book.

Institute for Experiential Education Processing Quiz[*]

by Steve Simpson, Buzz Bocher, and Dan Miller

This quiz consists of 12 scenarios, each followed by multiple-choice answers. Read each scenario and choose the answer that comes closest to the way you would process or debrief the experience. There are no right or wrong answers, so do not analyze the choices in terms of a "best" answer. Just choose the response that comes nearest to the way that you would actually handle the situation. There may be some scenarios where none of the options describe how you would process the experience;

---

[*] This quiz is copyrighted, but we certainly invite readers to photocopy the quiz and use it with facilitator trainings. If you could acknowledge the source when you use it, we would appreciate it.

there may be some scenarios where you would like to combine two or more answers. For purposes of the quiz, you are limited to one response per question. Pick the answer that seems better than the others. (Blank score sheets can be photocopied from p. 53.)

Score Sheet No. 1											
1.	2.	3.	4.	5.	6.	7.	8.	9.	10.	11.	12.

You are a high school civics teacher with 10 students volunteering at local nonprofit agencies as part of their grade for a course. The agencies include the Salvation Army, a hospital, a local nature center, the YMCA, and the Boys and Girls Club. On the first day of class, you assign each student to an agency that matches his or her interests. The directors of these agencies are expecting a call from the students, and it is the students' responsibility to initiate contact, find out about their volunteer opportunities, and perform 25 hours of service.

a. On the first day of class, you tell students that service learning is the link between academic training and the real world. You stress that their projects are civic responsibility put to practice. You give students journals and tell them their grade will be based on the connections they discover between course content and the volunteer experience. You will collect journals at the end of the semester.

b. You do not link a specific course assignment to the volunteer experience, but at 4, 8, and 12 weeks into the semester you dedicate a class period to talking about their experiences. You ask students questions about the challenges, frustrations, and accomplishments of their volunteer assignments and how the experiences relate to course lectures and reading assignments.

c. On the first day of class, you ask students to keep a journal about their volunteer experiences. You intentionally offer no suggestions about journal content. Then 4, 8, and 12 weeks into the semester, you have students read excerpts from their journals aloud to the class. You give the students opportunities to ask each other questions.

d. You do not link a specific course assignment to the volunteer experience, nor do you have formal discussions of the volunteer experiences. You trust that the significance of the experiences will be self-evident to the students, and that they will benefit from the non-classroom experiences without talking about them in class.

You are the freshman orientation coordinator for a local college. Part of your job is to lead a group of 15 incoming freshman on a 4-hour hike to the top of a mountain peak near campus. While there won't be any technical climbing, the route will challenge their abilities and endurance. The sun is shining, and the vistas from the summit should be beautiful.

a. Your only introduction to the hike is to state that it will be difficult and will take about 4 hours for the round trip. When the group reaches the summit, you bring the students together in a circle and ask them questions about the difficulties of the hike and the successful ascent. You follow up by asking them if the hike has any analogies to their upcoming freshman year in school.

b. Your only introduction to the hike is to state that it will be difficult and will take about 4 hours for the round trip. When the group reaches the summit, you bring the students together in a circle and pull out a bag of snacks. You tell the students they must make one comment about the hike before they get a treat. After going around the circle, you sit back and trust that the atmosphere of the experience and the close proximity of people in the circle will initiate an interesting conversation.

c. Your only introduction to the hike is to state that it will be difficult and will take about 4 hours for the round trip. When the group reaches the summit, you do nothing to disrupt the beauty of the vista and the sense of accomplishment. When you sense that interest is waning, you lead the group back down the mountain.

d. Prior to starting the hike, you discuss the challenges of pursuing a college degree. Then just before you start the ascent, you ask students to think of the step-by-step hike up the mountain as a metaphor for the upcoming school year. You suggest that like hiking up a mountain, the freshman year will be fun, but will also be difficult and that sometimes they will want to quit and go home. It will take perseverance to accomplish the ultimate goal.

You are the freshman orientation coordinator for a local college who last week took a group of freshman on a 4-hour hike up a mountain. The view from the top of the mountain was so beautiful that you take six friends on the same hike.

a. Prior to the start of the hike, you sit your friends down and tell them that the hike will be a challenge. But then you suggest that the challenge makes hiking up a mountain a metaphor for life. Good things in life do not come easy, nor does the sense of accomplishment in reaching the top of the mountain come easy.

b. Your only introduction to the hike is to state that it will be difficult and that it will take about 4 hours for the round trip. Your friends and you reach the summit. When you get to the top, you ask your friends to get in a circle. Then you hand out a snack and make a comment about a difficult stretch of the ascent. Then you ask them what they thought of the hike, trusting that the atmosphere of the experience and the proximity of people within the circle will initiate a conversation about the challenge.

c. Your only introduction to the hike is to state that it will be difficult and that it will take about 4 hours for the round trip. Your friends and you reach the summit. When you get to the top, you do nothing to disrupt the magic of the moment. You let your friends enjoy the view and, when you sense that their interest is waning, suggest heading back down.

d. Your only introduction to the hike is to state that it will be difficult and that it will take about 4 hours for the round trip. Your friends and you reach the summit. When you get to the top, you ask your friends to get in a circle. You then ask them questions about the difficulties of the hike. You also ask them if the hike has any analogies to anything that is happening to them in their everyday lives.

You are a director of a lakeside summer camp for children from families with low income. At the beginning of the season, you have a 9-day staff training before any of the kids arrive. Staff training culminates with an overnight camping trip, and the tradition of the trip is to wake up before dawn and quietly watch the sunrise.

a. You don't say anything prior to sunrise, but once the sun is fully above the horizon, you gather the staff together in a circle and spread out a deck of processing cards (50 different cards with evocative pictures on them). Then you ask each staff member to pick out and describe the card that best summarizes his or her impressions of the staff training just completed.

b. You do nothing before or after the sunrise. You simply let the dawn speak for itself.

c. Throughout staff training you have repeatedly described camp as "a new dawn" for a lot of the kids who come to camp. Most have never been to camp, many have spent little or no time in nature, some have no big brother/big sister types to serve as positive role models. Just prior to the sun coming up, you once more remind everyone that camp is "a new dawn."

d. You don't say anything prior to sunrise, but once the full ball of the sun is above the horizon, you gather the staff together in a circle and ask them about their concerns as they enter "the dawn" of a new camp season.

You are a trainer for a large corporation. One of your jobs is to take all new hires, regardless of their position in the company, through a day of generic orientation. One purpose of orientation is to promote interdepartmental cooperation, so you have the group of 24 new employees participate in a couple of group challenges/initiatives. Because the group is too large for one of the challenges, you divide it into two sub-groups before giving directions. The two groups will remain in the same room as they independently solve the identical challenge. Intentionally you say nothing about whether the sub-groups should work together, work independently, or compete with each other.

a. You do not introduce the initiative with a story line, but on their own, the two teams joke that the other team is the company's major competitor. From this banter, you decide that participants understand cooperation and competition in the corporate world, so once both teams complete the initiative, you take a 15-minute break and trust that participants will independently reflect on the activity.

b. Twice during the instructions to the initiative you state explicitly that the purpose of the day is promote a spirit of interdepartmental cooperation. Furthermore, the story line for the initiative reinforces the theme of cooperation, because you tell the group that each person should think of himself or herself as a representative from a different division within the company working with the other divisions to get a product to the customer as quickly as possible. Because cooperation is stated so strongly during the initial instructions, you do not bring it up after the challenge is completed.

c. You do not introduce the initiative with a story line, but on their own, the two teams joke that the other team is the company's major competitor. Immediately after the two groups complete the task, you state the obvious point that the success of each group depends upon cooperation. With the two groups back together in a single circle, you ask them to explain what led them to assume the other group was a competitor. You ask whether anyone considered bringing the two groups together, and if so, what it was that kept him or her from speaking up. You then ask follow-up questions about the success of the activity and the values of both cooperation and competition.

d. You do not introduce the initiative with a story line, but on their own, the two teams joke that the other team is the company's major competitor. Immediately after the two groups complete the task, you put people in groups of four (two from each sub-group) and ask them to talk about the group dynamics during the initiative.

You are an elementary school teacher. Your students pick up litter in the schoolyard and plant a flower garden on a small plot of land behind the school.

a. You introduce the schoolyard projects by saying that the class is going to make the school a better place to be. After the kids finish the projects and wash up, you gather them together in a circle and ask a series of questions on the theme of "think globally, act locally."

b. You introduce the schoolyard projects by saying that the class is going to make the school a better place to be. Based upon the total engagement of the students during the litter pick-up and the gardening, you decide not to talk about the projects and instead let each student reflect on his or her own.

c. You introduce the schoolyard projects by saying that the class is going to make the school a better place to be. After the kids finish the projects and wash up, you go back to the classroom and ask each student to draw a picture about what they learned from the experience. After drawing time is over, you let each student explain his or her picture, then you hang them all up on a classroom bulletin board.

d. The theme for the week in class is civic responsibility and community service. For the past four days, you have talked about the students' responsibility to their families and their school. Just before going outside, you again lecture about community service. All students understand, prior to the projects, that the litter pickup and the flower gardens are examples of putting an important classroom topic into practice.

You are a naturalist at a local nature center. You have just taken a group of high school students on a 2-hour hike along the center's marsh trail. The group saw deer, geese, and muskrats. The highlight of the trip was observing an active eagle nest through binoculars.

a. After the hike is completed, you do nothing, believing that the opportunity to watch an active eagle nest is so significant that it will leave a lasting impression.

b. After the hike is completed, you ask the students to take 10 minutes to write in their journals, then give students the opportunity to read from their journal entries.

c. After the hike is completed, you gather the students together in a circle and ask them questions about what had to have happened over the past 30 years to allow them to watch eagles, a bird once listed as a threatened species. You also ask them to express their feelings about seeing a bird that was once rare to the area.

d. Prior to the start of the hike, you describe the local political battles that were fought to have the nature center's four hundred acres set aside as a nature preserve. You explain the demise and the subsequent rebound of the eagle population in the region. You state that because of previous environment efforts, they get to see an eagle nest today (something not possible only 15 years earlier). Then you ask them to think, while on the hike, about their own potential contributions to the environmental movement.

You are a high school physical education teacher. Your class spends two class periods on your school's new climbing wall. (The climbing wall simulates rock climbing inside the school's gymnasium.) After instructions on the use of the wall and an hour of training on belay techniques, students take turns climbing and belaying.

   a. With 15 minutes left before you send the students to the showers, you gather the group in a circle and let each person say whatever he or she wants about climbing.

   b. With 15 minutes left before you send the students to the showers, you gather the group together in a circle and ask them questions about the value of recreational pursuits and physical activity.

   c. Your lengthy instructions on the use of the wall include a lecture about the role of physical education classes, emphasizing that the climbing instructions are not so much a few hours of exercise, but an introduction to a recreation activity that could provide a lifetime of physical fitness and productive leisure. At the end of the introduction lecture, you ask students to consider, while climbing, if rock climbing is an activity they will want to do in their free time.

   d. After of session of climbing, you simply send the students to the locker room to shower, confident that the uniqueness of the experience will excite many students about outdoor recreation.

You take a group of 10 adults to a local ropes and challenge course. All are individuals dealing with alcohol addiction. The goal of your program is to relate the challenge of the ropes course to the challenge of living a life of sobriety. The course has several high elements, which include a catwalk, a dangle-duo, and a pamper pole. (High elements of a ropes course are individual challenges in which participants climb 25+ feet in the air.) The participants are belayed by the ropes course staff, not fellow participants.

a. After completing the high elements, you ask the participants to get into groups of two and talk to each other about the day. After 10 minutes, you get everyone together, and each pair gives the rest of the group a summary of their 10-minute talk.

b. Prior to starting the high elements, you tell the group that asking for help on the ropes course is similar to asking for help with their addictions. Often the difference between success and failure is knowing when to ask for help.

c. After completing the high elements, you gather the group together in a circle and ask them about the difficulties of the ropes course. You follow with questions about whether there were any comparisons between the challenges of a ropes course and the challenges of maintaining sobriety.

d. After completing the high elements, you do nothing, trusting that the excitement and challenge of the high elements will make a lasting impact on the lives of the participants.

You are on the last day of a 5-day canoe trip with six boys. They are 13- and 14-years-old. They all have committed minor crimes (vandalism, petty theft, etc.) and have been identified as at-risk youth. They are on the canoe trip because either their parents or a local social services organization encouraged them to go. The trip has not been a smooth one. There has been lots of arguing, a fist fight between two participants, and threats of running away. Still the boys learned to paddle a canoe and cook meals for each other.

a. When you are about an hour away from the end of the trip, you have the boys pull the canoes to shore and come together in a circle. You ask them to review the successes and the mistakes of the past few days. You follow this review by asking them what they learned on the trip that will be useful once they get home.

b. Prior to the start of the trip, you tell the boys that the trip will be hard. In fact, you predicted events well, saying that there will be arguments, complaining, and a desire to pack up and go home. You also tell them that if they can succeed on a canoe trip, they can succeed with the problems they are facing in their daily lives. Since you hammer this theme prior to and during the trip, you feel no need to discuss it again at the end of the trip.

c. When you are about an hour away from the end of the trip, you have the boys pull the canoes to shore and let them stretch their legs for the last time. Before reboarding the canoes, you tell them that they are almost back to the cars and encourage them to paddle the last hour with little or no talking.

d. When you are about an hour away from the end of the trip, you have the boys pull the canoes to shore. You gather them in a circle and give each of them a last chance to say whatever is on his mind.

You are director of a municipal park and recreation department and have a full-time university student intern for 15 weeks. During the last week of internship, you take her to a city council meeting where a proposal for a $4 million swimming pool complex is on the agenda. After you formally present your proposal to the council, a heated debate occurs. About half of the council thinks the pool is needed; about half thinks it is a luxury that cannot be afforded. As expected, nothing is decided, and the topic is carried over to future meetings.

a. On the drive to the council meeting, you tell the intern what to watch for during the meeting. You ask her to determine what parts of the proposal are popular with council members and what parts are unpopular. You also ask that she try to determine which members of the council wield the most influence, which members listen to reason, and which members are the swing votes to determine whether the pool proposal passes or fails.

b. While traveling in the car after the council meeting, you wait for the intern to bring up the subject of the meeting. After 5 minutes of silence, you still do nothing, trusting that the intern is reflecting on her own about the meeting.

c. You did not prompt the student before the meeting, but traveling in the car after the council meeting, you ask the intern what her immediate reactions are. You also encourage her to jot down her thoughts about the meeting, so the two of you can talk more about it in the morning.

d. You did not prompt the student before the meeting, but traveling in the car after the council meeting, you ask if she could tell which parts of the proposal were popular with council members and which parts were unpopular. You also ask if she could tell which members seemed to wield the most influence, which members listened to reason, and which members were the swing votes to determine whether the pool proposal passes or fails.

You are an instructor for a community education course titled "Tai Chi for Seniors." The course meets once a week for 10 weeks. Fifteen participants register; the age range is 55 to 70. The goals of the class are 1) to teach a tai chi routine of 24 movements, 2) to help seniors maintain or enhance flexibility, and 3) to teach a low-impact exercise that seniors can do on a daily basis.

a. During the first class, you take the group through a series of short, stretching exercises and introduce the first three forms. With 10 minutes left in class, you ask everyone to sit on the floor or in a chair and quietly rest, meditate, or reflect on the class. After 9 minutes, you ask people to slowly leave their meditative states and stand up. You thank them and say that you look forward to next week.

b. During the first class, you take the group through a series of short, stretching exercises and introduce the first three forms. With 10 minutes left in class, you gather people in a group and ask 1) what they know about Tai Chi, 2) why they signed up for the course, and 3) what their current exercise routine is.

c. You begin the first class by explaining that in China, Hong Kong, and Taiwan small groups of elderly Chinese gather each morning to do Tai Chi. You explain that most of these senior citizens did not begin Tai Chi until they retired, but that they believe a daily regimen of gently moving muscles and circulating blood is important for good health and long life. After taking the group through stretching exercises and the first three forms, you thank them and say that you look forward to next week.

d. During the first class, you take the group through a series of short, stretching exercises and introduce the first three forms. With 15 minutes left in class, you ask everyone to sit on the floor or in a chair and quietly rest, mediate, or reflect for 5 minutes. For the last 10 minutes, you gather people in a circle and ask them to share what went through their minds while they sat quietly.

Scoring the Quiz

After taking the quiz, you should have a score sheet that looks like the one shown below:

Sample Score Sheet No. 1											
1.	2.	3.	4.	5.	6.	7.	8.	9.	10.	11.	12.
b	a	c	d	c	a	d	a	b	d	c	a

Now there is a two-step procedure to get the score into a format that can be used for interpretation. To start out, you should have a follow-up score sheet that looks like Score Sheet No. 2 (blank score sheets can be photocopied from p. 54). For step one, the answers on Score Sheet No. 1 need to be circled on Score Sheet No. 2.

Score Sheet No. 2	1.	2.	3.	4.	5.	6.	7.	8.	9.	10.	11.	12.	Totals
Row A	a	d	a	c	b	d	d	c	b	b	a	c	(A)
Row B	b	a	d	d	c	a	c	b	c	a	d	b	(B)
Row C	c	b	b	a	d	c	b	a	a	d	c	d	(C)
Row D	d	c	c	b	a	b	a	d	d	c	b	a	(D)

For example, the answers on Sample Score Sheet No. 1 would appear as shown on Sample Score Sheet No. 2. Note that the letters (a, b, c, d) are jumbled for each of the questions, so it is important that scores are transferred carefully. After the letters for each answer have been circled, count the number of answers in each of the four horizontal rows (Rows A, B, C, D). In the example, Row A has two (2) responses, Row B has five (5), Row C has three (3), and Row D has two (2). The results are recorded in the far right-hand column.

© 2006, Institute for Experiential Education, *The Processing Pinnacle*, Wood 'N' Barnes Publishing

Sample Score Sheet No. 2

	1.	2.	3.	4.	5.	6.	7.	8.	9.	10.	11.	12.	Totals
Row A	a	d	a	c	b	d	(d)	c	(b)	b	a	c	2 (A)
Row B	(b)	(a)	d	(d)	(c)	(a)	c	b	c	a	d	b	5 (B)
Row C	c	b	b	a	d	c	b	(a)	a	(d)	(c)	d	3 (C)
Row D	d	c	(c)	b	a	b	a	d	d	c	b	(a)	2 (D)

Finally, step two of transferring the scores is to take the totals of the four horizontal rows and place these numbers on Score Sheet No. 3 (blank score sheets can be photocopied from p. 55).

Score Sheet No. 3: The Processing Matrix

C	B
D	A

For example, the hypothetical person with the quiz results shown in the sample chose "A" two times, "B" five times, "C" three times, and "D" two times. Therefore the grid should look like Sample Score Sheet No. 3.

Sample Score Sheet No. 3: The Processing Matrix	
3	5
C	B
2	2
D	A

Interpreting the Quiz Results

With Score Sheet No. 3 filled out, you are ready to read chapter 5 of the book and begin to interpret the quiz results. At this point, anyone who takes the quiz can only see whether he or she favors some quadrants over others. Our recommendation is for the reader to take his or her filled-in Score Sheet No. 3 and use it as a bookmark while reading chapter 5. Then as each quadrant is defined, the reader can look at the quiz results and respond, "Yes, that sounds like me," or "No, that isn't how I see processing at all."

Score Sheet No. 1

1.	2.	3.	4.	5.	6.	7.	8.	9.	10.	11.	12.

Score Sheet No. 1

1.	2.	3.	4.	5.	6.	7.	8.	9.	10.	11.	12.

Score Sheet No. 2

	1.	2.	3.	4.	5.	6.	7.	8.	9.	10.	11.	12.	Totals
Row A	a	d	a	c	b	d	d	c	b	b	a	c	(A)
Row B	b	a	d	d	c	a	c	b	c	a	d	b	(B)
Row C	c	b	b	a	d	c	b	a	a	d	c	d	(C)
Row D	d	c	c	b	a	b	a	d	d	c	b	a	(D)

Score Sheet No. 3: The Processing Matrix	
C	B
D	A

Score Sheet No. 3: The Processing Matrix	
C	B
D	A

The Processing Matrix and Interpretation of the Quiz

Processing is like an eddy in the river.
An eddy is the most intimate spot from which to observe
the flow of the river, but the novice paddler needs training
before he can maneuver his canoe out of the active current
and into that quiet place.

As you read chapter 5, it would be best to have the final results of the quiz from chapter 4 alongside. It will take a few pages to get there, but the eventual purpose of this chapter is to interpret the quiz score. First, however, the chapter presents some background information that will help make sense of the quiz results. The final numbers from the quiz should appear in the 2 x 2 matrix grid, looking something like this:

Sample Score Sheet No. 3: The Processing Matrix	
3	5
C	B
2	2
D	A

Finding Balance in Processing

Experiential educators constantly try to find the balance between overprocessing and underprocessing a group. One part of this balance is identifying the appropriate amount of time for processing. This is when facilitators ask themselves such questions as "Should processing for this activity last 5 minutes or 25 minutes?" or "Should I ask one more question with this group or cut off discussion now?" Obviously, the number of minutes taken for processing is important. Anyone who has watched a processor begin well, then lose a group with a processing session that is a half hour of rhetoric and redundant questions, realizes that knowing when to stop is almost as important as knowing what to do.

Still, balance in processing is more than time management. It also is the extent to which a facilitator controls the direction of the processing. From this perspective, when a facilitator gives participants, especially inexperienced participants, too much freedom during a processing session, underprocessing can occur. If participants are given responsibility for the success of a processing session before they are ready to handle it, the session will most likely fail. Discussions will lack focus and include pointless digression; the important lessons of an experience will not come to light.

Conversely, overprocessing can occur when a facilitator continues to maintain control of the processing even when participants have developed the skills to do some of the processing on their own. As a result, processing is restricted only to topics deemed important by the facilitator, and participants are not allowed to bring up worthwhile issues that are important to them.

The difficulty with finding the appropriate balance is that there is no single right amount of facilitator control. As with so much in experiential education, it is situational. A group that is naturally reflective may be able to process on its own, whereas a group entirely new to experiential education may need extensive guidance. Also, a group that may be able to assume responsibility for the

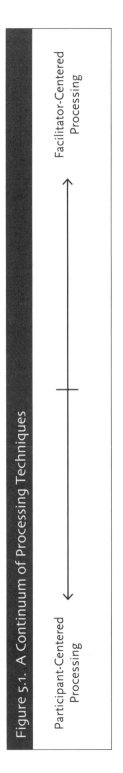

Figure 5.1. A Continuum of Processing Techniques

Participant-Centered
Processing

Facilitator-Centered
Processing

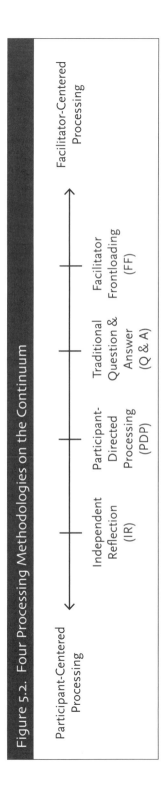

Figure 5.2. Four Processing Methodologies on the Continuum

Participant-Centered
Processing

Independent
Reflection
(IR)

Participant-
Directed
Processing
(PDP)

Traditional
Question &
Answer
(Q & A)

Facilitator
Frontloading
(FF)

Facilitator-Centered
Processing

processing after one kind of activity may need help after another kind. The amount of facilitator control depends on the topics being discussed. A group that is able to process on its own when the lessons of the activity are obvious may need facilitator guidance when the lessons are not readily apparent. In other words, a responsible facilitator is continually trying to figure out when to assume responsibility for the direction of the processing and when to encourage the participants to lead the processing.

A Processing Continuum

One way of looking at the extent to which a facilitator controls a processing session is to think of processing as a continuum.[1] At one end of the continuum is processing in which the facilitator or educator retains total control over the direction of the processing. This could be referred to as facilitator-centered processing. At the opposite end of the continuum is processing in which the facilitator relinquishes control of the processing and lets participants process (or not process) in any way that they see fit. This would be participant-centered processing. Processing where control of the processing is shared between facilitators and participants lies somewhere in between the two extremes (see Figure 5.1).

With such a continuum, various processing methodologies can be placed in relation to each other, the most facilitator-centered at one end of the spectrum and the least facilitator-centered on the other end. For example, **Facilitator Frontloading** (FF) would reside at the facilitator-centered end of the spectrum (see Figure 5.2). Frontloading is explicitly stating the purpose of an activity even before the activity takes place.[2] This is done so that the purpose is foremost on participants' minds as they progress through the action. And because the purpose is on their minds during the action, reflection occurs throughout the activitiy and not just afterwards. For example, a facilitator may tell a group of people undergoing therapy for alcohol addiction that each step of a difficult hike is going be like one step toward sobriety. Then when participants complain halfway through that the hike route is too hard, it immediately registers with them that giving up on the hike is analogous to giving up on their treatment.* In terms of process-ing, this means that the outcomes and lessons of the experience have been predetermined and chosen solely by the facilitator. If frontloading works as intended, the participants are reflecting on their actions throughout the experience, and the themes of that reflection are the themes that the facilitator introduced.

At the opposite end of the continuum from facilitator-centered processing would be the intentional absence of formal process-ing. Instead of a facilitator guiding a processing session, each person within the group is left to process on his or her own. In adventure programing, this **Independent Reflection** (IR) is often called "Mountains Speak for Themselves," an evocative phrase that recognizes that some situations are so exceptional that the participants are in a position to process entirely on their own.[3] For example, a natural vista on a backpacking trip may be so stunning that the best thing the facilitator can do is keep his or her mouth shut and let the participants take in the beauty of the moment.

In between Facilitator Frontloading and Independent Reflection on the continuum are processing methods that require input from both the facilitator and the participants to be successful. One example of this middle ground would be **Traditional Ques-tion and Answer** (Q & A). Traditional Q & A is the common debriefing practice of having a discussion immediately after a group completes the action component of an experience. While Q & A requires contributions from both the facilitator and the participants, it is the facilitator who chooses the questions and serves as gatekeeper for the discussion. The facilitator, while not dictatorial, hangs on to a fair amount of the control, so Q & A would not be placed dead center on the continuum. It would show up on the spectrum as more facilitator-centered than par-ticipant-centered.

---

* The hike-is-like-sobriety example is a good one, because frontloading very often is couched in a metaphor. Metaphoric frontloading is dis-cussed in detail in chapter 7.

Finally tucked between Independent Reflection and Traditional Question and Answer is **Participant-Directed Processing** (PDP). Participant-Directed Processing includes processing techniques that are a formal part of the experience, but the direction of the discussion and reflection is determined by the participants, not the facilitator. The most commonly used example of PDP is journaling. In journaling, the facilitator asks the participants to take a few minutes to put their thoughts about an experience to paper. Even if the individuals come together as a group to discuss those journal entries, the content of the discussion is based upon the writings of the participants, not the impressions of the facilitator.

A second good example of PDP is concept maps. These are pictures or flowcharts drawn by participants to describe or summarize a recent learning experience. Usually the pictures are drawn in groups of three to five participants, so a group of fifteen may end up with five different concept maps, each one a different symbolic representation of the experience just shared.

And a third example of PDP is processing cards. Processing cards are a collection of words or symbols that help participants develop their own metaphors for the experience just completed. We, for example, have developed Chiji Processing Cards, a deck of 48 playing cards with different images on them. The images, such as a lighthouse, shattered pottery, and a sunset, are designed to evoke feelings and reflections about the experience that might otherwise not be realized. A facilitator can ask each participant to pick a card that best describes his or her role in the group. One participant may pick a picture of a wrapped gift because she feels that she has strengths to share with the group, but has yet to open up. Another may pick a picture of a thunderstorm, explaining to the group that he sometimes charges into a challenge without thinking about how his actions affect everyone else. With processing cards, the facilitator establishes the method of processing, but the large number of cards and the range of interpretations for each card give the participants considerable freedom in interpreting the experience for themselves. Both concept maps and processing cards are described in detail in appendix A of this book.

It should be noted that three of the four methodologies described here are not concepts originated by us. Facilitator Frontloading, Traditional Question and Answer, and Independent Reflection all have direct equivalents in Outward Bound literature.[4] Outward Bound (OB), long a leader in adventure programing, also was a pioneer in processing the outdoor experience. In OB vernacular, Facilitator Frontloading is called the Metaphoric Curriculum Model, Traditional Question and Answer is called Outward Bound Plus, and as already mentioned, Independent Reflection is called Mountains Speak for Themselves.[*] The one category that is of our own creation is Participant-Directed Processing. It was introduced by us because we thought that the gap between Traditional Question and Answer and Independent Reflection was too wide. There is a big difference between a facilitator controlling a question-answer session and a facilitator deliberately choosing not to process at all. Between Q & A and IR are techniques where participants are required to formally process, but the direction of the processing is determined primarily by the participants rather than the facilitator. This is what we called PDP or Participant-Directed Processing.[5]

A Processing Matrix

The processing continuum described in Figure 5.2 does a good job of representing the level of *facilitator* involvement across a range of processing methodologies. What it does not do as well is depict the level and the type of *participant* involvement; on this point, representation is incomplete. Even though the continuum has one end described as "participant-centered," it does not differentiate between individual reflection and group-based reflection. Individual reflection, or processing that is done

---

[*] In our own early writings about processing, we used the descriptive Outward Bound terms to name the three categories (Metaphoric Curriculum Model, etc.). Over time, however, our thinking changed enough from the original OB literature that we thought it more accurate to use the more generic terms of Facilitator Frontloading, Traditional Question and Answer, and Independent Reflection.

alone and often internally, is more personal than any group session. For example, individual reflection may be linked to life experiences that a person does not want to discuss openly with others. It also may be a serene reflection, a peaceful contemplation that actually would be disrupted by a lively group discussion. Group reflection, conversely, often has an enthusiastic banter that cannot be accomplished with only one person. The interaction between participants often elicits insights that no single person could have come up with on his or her own. Also group-based reflection is public, meaning that the facilitator and the group members learn what other people are thinking.

With the difference between individual reflection and group reflection in mind, we suggest that the continuum of processing techniques can be presented in a two-dimensional matrix (see Figure 5.3).

Figure 5.3. The Processing Matrix

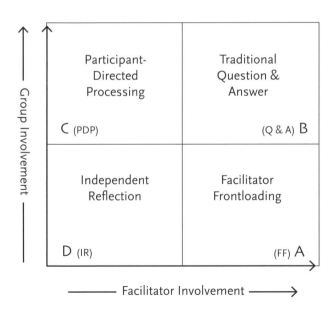

There are a couple of basic advantages to arranging processing methodologies in this format. First of all, the matrix creates a 2 x 2 representation in which the four methodologies can be viewed not only in terms of facilitator involvement or control (the x-axis), but also in terms of group involvement (the y-axis). For example, a facilitator not only needs to decide whether to put the onus of responsibility for processing on the participants; she must also decide whether she wants the participants to assume that responsibility as one large group or as individuals. If she wants the group to assume responsibility together, PDP-type activities are in order; if she wants individualistic reflection, IR-type techniques would be more applicable.

Anyone familiar with Situational Leadership will realize that this processing matrix mirrors Hershey and Blanchard's Situational Leadership model.[6] Hershey and Blanchard claim that leader-ship usually follows a progression, starting with a leader who initially makes decisions for a group and gradually delegates authority to the participants. The progression moves from an initial period of authoritarian leadership to a period where lead-er and participants lead together and maybe even to a situation where individuals, while still part of a group, are able to make decisions independent of both the leaders and the others in the group. The processing matrix does exactly the same thing, sug-gesting that processing follows a similar progression. Initially, participants of experiential education need to be taken by the hand when it comes to processing, later they can co-process as a group with a facilitator, and eventually they develop the skills to process independently as mature and reflective individuals.

A second advantage of the 2 x 2 matrix configuration is that the four boxes of the matrix offer facilitators a way to arrange their repertoire of processing techniques in an orderly way. For exam-ple, a ropes course facilitator might have six different process-ing activities that she frequently uses with the groups she serves (see Figure 5.4). Seventy percent of the time she conducts question and answer sessions, but on occasion she uses jour-naling, dyads,* processing cards, frontloading with metaphoric story lines, and sharing circles.

Figure 5.4. Processing Matrix with Techniques

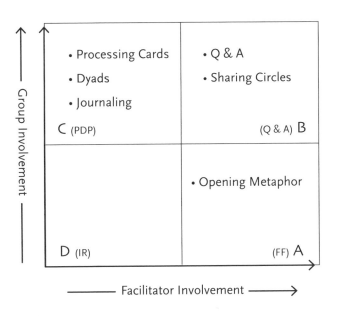

Group Involvement

- Processing Cards
- Dyads
- Journaling

C (PDP)

- Q & A
- Sharing Circles

(Q & A) B

- Opening Metaphor

D (IR)

(FF) A

Facilitator Involvement ⟶

It would not be difficult for this facilitator to place the various techniques into the quadrants where they best fit. For example, she might take a look at her matrix and conclude that metaphoric stories belong in the FF quadrant; question and answer, along with sharing circles, go in the Q & A quadrant; and journaling, dyads, and processing cards all fit best into PDP. The facilitator now has a visual representation of her processing repertoire. This facilitator then looks at the results and discovers that nearly all of her processing techniques have very high group involvement (i.e., they are in the upper two quadrants of Q & A and PDP). This is not surprising to her, because most of her programing emphasizes teamwork, but she decides that at least one approach in her processing repertoire should have a more Independent Reflection feel to it. Uncomfortable with the fact

---

* Dyads are participants breaking into groups of two or three to discuss an activity. Sharing circles are a technique in which the facilitator asks one question and participants, seated in a circle, each take turns answering that one question. See appendix A for detailed information on dyads.

that she has nothing that stresses individualized processing, she divides her journaling exercise into two distinct techniques. One she calls mandatory journaling, where she 1) sets aside time specifically for journaling, 2) determines the subject of the journal assignment, and 3) culminates the processing by bringing the participants together to read journal excerpts to each other. The other technique she calls self-initiated journaling, where she simply hands out a small journal to each participant at the beginning of the day and hopes that some of them will use it. Such an arrangement seems to her a more balanced approach (see Figure 5.5).

Figure 5.5. Balancing the Techniques

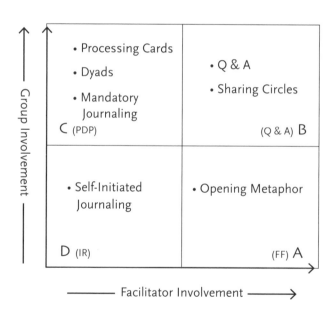

Interpreting the Processing Quiz

Now that you have an understanding of the Processing Matrix, it is time to pull out scores from the quiz and interpret the results.* With an understanding of the four squares of the quadrant, it is now possible to identify personal processing tendencies. For example, a person can see whether she leans toward IR or repeatedly gravitates toward Q & A. Three different ways to interpret quiz results are described below:

Interpretation No. 1: General Observations

The most direct way to look at the quiz scores recorded in the four boxes is to see whether you have a tendency toward a particular quadrant. Once you know that the four boxes represent FF, Q & A, PDP, and IR, you can see how your answers correlate with these various techniques. How, for example, would you answer the following questions:

- Are you heavy in one of the four categories? Are you fairly evenly distributed in two, three, or four categories? In other words, do your quiz results tend toward a certain level of facilitator control and/or group involvement, or do your results put you all over the place? Some facilitators, for example, like Q & A and do not feel comfortable with turning full control over to the participants. Others might, on principle, shy away from formal processing and, therefore, are high in IR.

- Did any of the categories have zero points (any quadrant you didn't pick even once)? If so, can you explain why?

- Did the quiz results correctly reflect what you consider to be your processing preferences? Why or why not?

---

* This section of chapter 5 is written in second person. While inconsistent with the rest of the book, it is the easiest way to speak directly to the reader about interpreting his or her test scores.

- Why do you have a processing preference? Is it your personality? Is it because a specific leadership style works best with your particular clientele? Is it because you have faith in specific processing techniques?

For example, Figure 5.6 shows a typical range of scores, with two points in quadrant A, five points in quadrant B, three points in quadrant C, and two points in quadrant D. The experiential educator might conclude that these scores are a correct reflection of his processing. While he uses Q & A most of the time, he does, in principle, believe that processing should vary with the abilities of the group. With a group he does not know well, he uses Q & A as safe and dependable middle ground, but when he understands the personality and abilities of a group, he often alters his leadership and his processing techniques to coincide with the group. Although he does not want to be authoritarian, he understands himself well enough to know that he has a hard time relinquishing all authority and delegating responsibility

Figure 5.6. Hypothetic Quiz Score

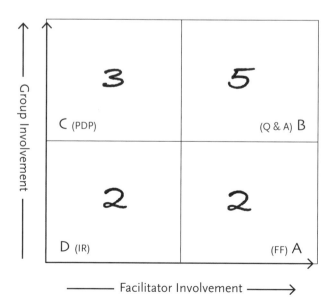

to the group. Being high in the Q & A quadrant, therefore, makes sense.

Interpretation No. 2: Situational Processing

A second way to interpret the quiz scores is to go back and review the 12 scenarios of the quiz. As you look at the various scenarios, do you think that the specifics of each scenario caused you to process in a particular way? For example, did you tend to use one type of processing technique with children and another with adults? Did you lean toward IR when the purpose of the activity was recreational, but process more prescriptively when the purpose of the activity was educational or therapeutic? Did you use one kind of processing technique when the program lasted only one day and another when the program was a full semester in length? In other words, are you a situational processor? By observing how you answered each of the questions, you might be able to identify the triggers that led you to process one way or another.

If you want to look seriously at situational processing, retake the quiz. It is worthwhile to see whether your answers change now that you know that the various answers correspond to the four categories of FF, Q & A, PDP, and IR.

Interpretation No. 3: Critique the Quiz

To be honest, the quiz is a tool to get experiential educators to think about their processing tendencies. The four possible answers are forced to fit the four categories of the Processing Matrix. In the real world, however, processing and the myriad of processing techniques are fluid. The matrix offers a framework from which to visualize the range of processing techniques, but that does not mean that facilitators methodically jump from box to box like children playing hopscotch. Facilitators hone their processing skills in order to glide from technique to technique and bring their participants to new knowledge and awareness.

A third way to learn from the quiz is to go back to the 12 scenarios, but this time disregard the four multiple-choice answers—just consider the situation in the scenario and determine, without the restrictions imposed by a multiple-choice quiz, how to process for the situation.* For example, in the civics teacher scenario with the service learning projects, you might frontload the experience, require journals, and still talk about the experiences periodically throughout the semester. It is not one method or the other; it is several.

We know, from using the quiz at experiential education workshops, that some facilitators are frustrated by the restrictions imposed by the multiple-choice format. Here's a chance to ignore the restrictions and come up with processing solutions that exceed any offered by the quiz.

---

* Another option for using the quiz is to not use the multiple choice answers at all. Educators could give facilitators-in-training three or four of the scenarios (without the multiple choice answers) and ask them how they would process the experiences. The scenarios would then no longer serve as a lead-in to the processing matrix, but could be an interesting tool to initiate discussion about processing methods.

The Processing Pinnacle

Section Three describes the Processing Pinnacle, the model for which this book is named. Chapter 6 briefly explains the model in a general sense, and the four subsequent chapters explain the four components of the Processing Pinnacle in detail. The four components are the same four components introduced in the processing continuum and the Processing Matrix (Facilitator Frontloading, Traditional Question and Answer, Participant-Directed Processing, and Independent Reflection).

Chapters 6 and 11 bring back Yangtze and McKinley, the two characters introduced in chapter 1. In chapter 6, they discuss their initial reactions to the Processing Pinnacle and, in effect, personify the comments that we have heard from people who have attended our presentations about the Pinnacle at experiential education conferences. In chapter 11, Yangtze and McKinley return to summarize the underlying concepts of the model and show how experiential educators might incorporate these concepts into their own facilitation.

SECTION THREE

The Processing Pinnacle

*Processing is like climbing a mountain in foul weather.
It is an extraordinary moment if you are on the summit
when everything becomes clear.*

The Processing Pinnacle, the model that we are about to describe, was first presented in 1998 at the Midwest Symposium
on Therapeutic Recreation.[1] The session was not well received.
Attendees to the workshop did not like the hierarchical structure
of the mountain metaphor. They said that the model insulted
people who might never reach the summit. The symposium audience, mostly therapeutic recreation specialists, often worked
with individuals who have significant cognitive disabilities, and
the session participants felt that the Pinnacle established a goal
that their clients had no chance of achieving.

Because of the cool reception at the Midwest Symposium, we
put the Processing Pinnacle on hiatus for several years. Even
though controversy can add spice to a conference workshop,
controversy about the Processing Pinnacle, in the case of the
Midwest Symposium, did little more than divert attention
away from the concepts that the model was intended to highlight. It was an easy decision, at least temporarily, to keep the
contentious model out of facilitator training sessions. At least
temporarily...

---

* This statement is a misquote of Thoreau in *The Maine Woods*. The
actual quote is "If I wished to see mountain or other scenery under the
most favorable auspices, I would go to it in foul weather, so as to be there
when it cleared up; we are then in the most suitable mood, and nature is
the most fresh and inspiring."

Even though the three of us rarely discussed the Processing Pinnacle with others, it still served as a guide in our own work. The key point of the Pinnacle is that an overriding goal of processing is to move participants toward a high level of self-reflection. Other than this point, the Pinnacle, from our perspective, was not significantly different from the Processing Matrix. The Pinnacle and the Matrix have the same four categories presented in slightly different configurations. Yet, suggesting that Independent Reflection is an ultimate goal of experiential education, brings to the forefront that particular aspect of experiential education.

The Processing Pinnacle

So what is the Processing Pinnacle? The Processing Pinnacle is simply stacking the four categories of the Processing Matrix[*] one atop another (see Figure 6.1). Facilitator Frontloading is at the base, Traditional Question and Answer is at level two, Participant-Directed Processing is at level three, and Independent Reflection is at the top. The hierarchical structure is shown as a mountain peak, suggesting that reaching the summit of individual independent reflection is the ultimate goal. The Pinnacle's hierarchical depiction of processing does sacrifice the circular flow of the 2 x 2 Processing Matrix, but what is gained is a visual representation of a general overall goal for experiential education when it comes to processing.

Like the Matrix, the Processing Pinnacle suggests that quality experiential education gradually shifts responsibility for processing from facilitator to participants. Facilitator Frontloading is the most authoritarian; IR is the least. Traditional Q & A and PDP are somewhere in between. This, of course, is not neces-

---

[*] The Processing Matrix was explained in chapter 5. This current chapter and its thumbnail explanation of the Processing Pinnacle may be hard to understand without first reading about the Matrix. Readers who skipped chapter 5 may want to go back to it at this time and read the few paragraphs that explain the Matrix.

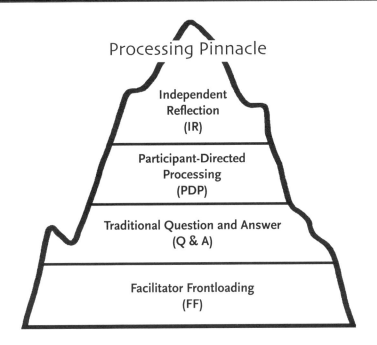

Figure 6.1. The Processing Pinnacle

Processing Pinnacle

Independent Reflection (IR)

Participant-Directed Processing (PDP)

Traditional Question and Answer (Q & A)

Facilitator Frontloading (FF)

sarily a smooth and continuous ascent. The route might have false summits.* It might travel straight up the steepest parts of the rock face; it might meander along, gradually zigzagging its way up the back side. Some people may begin at the very base of the mountain (i.e., FF); others may begin part way up (i.e., at Traditional Q & A). Some people may never reach the summit, but even for these people, the summit pokes out of the clouds as the ideal. The mountain is a common metaphor, and it seems to be one that is particularly appropriate for a profession with deep ties to outdoor recreation and outdoor education.

---

* False summits occur when people are so close to the mountain that they cannot see the real top. When they look up, they see directly above them a place that seems to be the top of the mountain—but when they get to that place, they realize that it is only a ledge or a knoll enroute to the true summit. A false summit might be a good place to rest—it might even be the goal of a group that never intended to go all the way to the top—but it's not the top of the mountain.

Implicit in the Processing Pinnacle is the concept that changes in the processing methodology coincide with changes in the primary reason for processing. At the base of the Pinnacle, the primary reason for processing is to reveal the lessons of a particular experiential education session. FF, for example, leaves nothing to chance when it comes to explaining the purpose of an experience. When a facilitator and his/her group move up the Processing Pinnacle, *the purpose of processing increasingly shifts away from making explicit predetermined goals and toward teaching people the skills for independent reflection, so when left to their own devices, they will process on their own.*

Teaching people the importance of reflection and providing them with techniques for effective reflection enhances the likelihood that all experiences, including those not overseen by a facilitator, will be educational. Helping people to achieve self-reflection is actually a form of transference. Transference is the ability of people to take the lessons of a formalized training session and generalize them to everyday life. The Processing Pinnacle states that part of independent learning is the ability to reflect on life's experiences, and part of experiential education is teaching people how to reflect on their own.

The audience at the Midwest Symposium on Therapeutic Recreation did not like a model that intimated that one kind of processing was better than another and that people who could process on their own were better than those who needed facilitator guidance for their processing. From our perspective, the Processing Pinnacle does not rank the value of processing techniques, nor does it judge people. The model does say that IR is more difficult than PDP, Q & A, and FF. IR is the ability of individuals to accomplish independently what normally requires help from others. This is hard. It is also worthwhile. IR is the end result of other processing methodologies, which lay the groundwork for worthwhile self-processing.

Six months have passed since Yangtze and McKinley sat at the campfire and discussed processing. They've just met up at the annual Association for Experiential Education conference and went together to a session about the Processing Pinnacle. Walking out of the session....

McKinley: What did you think of the session?

Yangtze: It was good and bad. The processing techniques that we did were pretty clever, and I will use some of them. But that model of the mountain was awful. I wanted to call the presenters on it, but then we ran out of time....

What? What are you smiling at?

McKinley: I thought the model was great. It synthesized my own thoughts about processing in a way I hadn't been able to do on my own. I'm smiling because I knew that if it worked for me, you probably wouldn't like it. I am sure that you don't like models in general, and I'm guessing that the Processing Pinnacle really drove you up the wall.

Yangtze: The Processing Pinnacle. Let me guess—a male came up with that name? I thought the whole concept was hierarchical and inflexible. It was just so male.

McKinley: What does that mean?

Yangtze: Male? You know what it means.

McKinley: Yeah, male in this case means logical, analytical, and orderly. I don't consider those things negative.

Yangtze: They are negative when we're talking about something as fluid as processing. Models are a lousy way to explain processing in the first place, and making a model that is hierarchical takes a bad idea and makes it worse.

McKinley: Oh, I disagree. The mountain as a metaphor for processing is excellent in so many ways. It offers a path, a clear goal, a challenge. The moment I saw the picture of the Processing Pinnacle, my mind went to strength, beauty, permanence, and the big picture. The actual drawing of the mountain they used in their presentation might have been a little cartoonish, but you won't even give the metaphor a chance. In your mind, the mountain is male and hierarchical, so it must be wrong. When I saw the mountain, I was hooked.

Yangtze: I love mountains almost as much as you do. It doesn't mean that mountains have anything to do with processing. Processing is ephemeral, intuitive, subtle—pretty much all of the things that mountains are not. There are two great metaphors in nature. One is the mountain. The other is the river. To me, processing is more like a river.

McKinley: Rivers are great, too—so I'll bite. Why is processing like a river?

Yangtze: Because it flows like a river. Sometimes the pace is fast and furious, and sometimes it is like a still, deep pool. A river gradually works its way to the sea, but the path it takes is winding. A paddler on the river will have different branches to take and different obstacles to avoid. If a paddler is inattentive, even for a moment, she might run up on a sand bar and bring progress to a stop.

McKinley: And nothing in that description of a river does me any good. So what if processing flows like a river? That's a pretty image, but it is not a model. It tells me nothing about being a better facilitator. A river metaphor suggests aimless meandering, whereas a mountain metaphor presents a plan. Start at the base of the mountain, then climb as far up as your skills allow. Plan a route, pick the right gear, have a goal, then gradually move toward that goal. Maybe experiential education flows like a river, but I don't need a metaphor to tell me that. What I need is a clear model to get me started on a viable path. When I go climbing, I don't always follow the route that I planned when I was on the ground. That doesn't mean the initial plan wasn't useful. It was the foundation from which I am able to deviate. That's all the Processing Pinnacle is—a logical step-by-step plan for conducting processing.

Yangtze: But it's a plan carved on a mountain—as if it's written in stone. Why does the plan have to be hierarchical, and why does it have to say that one technique is better than everything else?

McKinley: I'm surprised that you're complaining about the hierarchy. The Processing Pinnacle puts your freeform style of processing at the top. The very thing that you value the most, self-processing and maximum freedom for the participants, is the method that the Pinnacle presents as the ultimate goal. It says that you got it right.

Yangtze: I don't want to be right. Good processing isn't about right or wrong, best or worst. That's my point. I know putting Facilitator Frontloading and Traditional Question and Answer toward the bottom of the mountain doesn't make them bad, but it makes them less desirable than Independent Reflection. You're the question/answer man, which is low on the mountain, and I'm the let-people-reflect-on-their-own facilitator. Yet when we see a model that puts self-reflection on a pedestal, you are all for it, and I think it is awful.

Which processing techniques do you rely upon the most?

McKinley: That is kinda weird, isn't it? I don't mind the hierarchy because I don't see the top of the mountain as any more important than the base. In fact, it might be just the opposite. The kind of processing that I do is the foundation upon which less formal processing is built. A person needs the basics before undertaking more independent processing methods. The top represents the ultimate goal, but that doesn't make it better than the rest of the mountain. You are too hung up on the summit. If being on the top was all that mattered, the National Park Service would run trams to the top of Half Dome, the Grand Teton, and Mount Rainier, and everybody could get to the summit after a 15-minute gondola ride. But it doesn't work that way. Just like you can't plunk people on the top of a mountain and expect them to feel a sense of accomplishment, you can't just wave goodbye to people after a shared experience and expect them to process on their own. Processing is a process, and the Pinnacle offers a clear sequence for that process to occur.

Yangtze: Yeah, but it is so rigid.

McKinley: It has structure, but it's structure that I am looking for. Sometimes experiential education has so much flexibility that I don't know what's going on. What good is it to build up a repertoire of processing activities, but have no idea when to use one over another?

Yangtze: Maybe the sequence doesn't matter as much as you think. So what if you make a mistake and have people write in their journals when it would have been more effective to sit down and have a question and answer session? Trust your gut, use a little variety in techniques so it's not boring, and don't worry about everything being perfect. It's not going to be perfect anyway.

Do you sequence your favorite processing techniques?

McKinley: I appreciate what you are saying, but I still like an orderly progression. Start with a few clear metaphors, so people understand what they are supposed to learn, then gradually wean them from the facilitator's heavy hand. With my method, people don't get to the pinnacle of the mountain until they have the skills to handle the ascent. In fact, most don't get to the top at all, but that's okay. Better to be base camped halfway up the mountain than pushed to the top before they're ready. If things are too free flowing, some people will be sent adrift before they have the requisite skills to navigate on their own. I don't have a river analogy for "falling through the cracks," but that is what I want to avoid above all else. I want to make sure no one falls through the cracks.

Yangtze: That is the dilemma, isn't it? How to turn people free just at the right time. How to offer guidance without squashing individual freedom. You want people to climb the established path so no one gets lost. I'm encouraging people to take the less traveled fork of a river, even though I suspect some might not be ready to be off on their own.

McKinley: That's right. You're method works best for people who need your help the least. People who are naturally reflective will appreciate the freedom you afford. Those who are not reflective may not get the help they need. My method makes sure no one gets left behind, even if it means that the most capable won't get as far as they might have on their own. That's fine. If they have the mettle, they'll continue on their own after I'm done working with them.

Yangtze: If you haven't curbed their enthusiasm by your inflexible programing.

McKinley: Yeah, if that hasn't happened.

Yangtze: So that leaves us at the same place as we were after our campfire talk last summer. My style fits me, and your style fits you.

How would you describe your processing style?

Some folks benefit most from my style, and some folks from yours.

McKinley: Yeah, like the hundred paths up the mountain—a mountain metaphor, by the way.

Yangtze: I don't know the hundred paths up the mountain.

McKinley: It's a Hindu proverb, and it says we're both on the right track. There are hundreds of paths up the mountain, all leading in the same direction, so it doesn't matter which path you take. The only one wasting time is the one who runs around and around the mountain, telling everyone that his or her path is wrong.[2]

The Hammer*

*A facilitator's processing repertoire is like a tackle box.
A fisherman adds new and exotic pieces of equipment
to the box, but usually relies on the same one or two old
lures that he knows will catch fish.*

The next four chapters look at the categories of the Processing
Pinnacle in greater detail. This chapter will review Facilitator
Frontloading. Chapter 8 will offer tips on conducting Traditional
Question and Answer sessions. Chapter 9 looks at Participant-
Directed Processing, and chapter 10 winds up the detailed
discussions with a further look at Independent Reflection.

Explicit Goals and Objectives

Of all processing methods, the most explicit, the most authoritarian, is Facilitator Frontloading. With FF, the facilitator states
up front 1) what the participants are going to do and 2) why they
are going to do it. The method intentionally leaves no room for
doubt as to what is going to occur. The facilitators have specific
predetermined goals and objectives, and they make it a priority
to hammer home those goals and objectives before the action
component of the experience even begins. When done effectively, the participants are not only told of the goals and objectives before the action begins, but they also are cognizant of the
goals and objectives throughout the planned educational experience. Then when a lesson associated with the stated goals and

---

* One reviewer of the book felt that naming this chapter "The Hammer"
put Facilitator Frontloading in a negative light. This was not our inten-
tion. The hammer metaphor connotes a methodology that is explicit and
emphatic, certainly two characteristics that are sometimes needed.

objectives presents itself within an activity, the participants all recognize it for what it is.

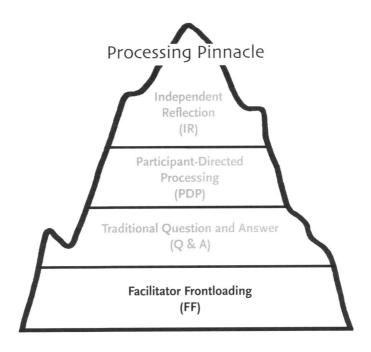

The example of FF already mentioned in this book is the group hike with individuals undergoing addiction treatment. The facilitator tells the group, before the hike begins, that the hike will be difficult and people will want to give up and turn around. He asks the group to think of the hike as a journey toward sobriety. Each step forward is analogous to another day without alcohol and drugs. Then during the hike, when members of the group tire and want to turn around, the metaphor of the hike is apparent to everyone.

Trained experiential educators see valuable lessons constantly and can bring these lessons to the attention of the participants through verbal explanations and question and answer sessions. FF is a tool to help participants see the lessons of an ongoing action well before the facilitator points them out.

Metaphors in Facilitator Frontloading

As mentioned in chapter 5, outdoor leadership often refers to Facilitator Frontloading as the Metaphoric Curriculum Model, pointing out that frontloading by the facilitator often includes metaphor. In other words, the educational experience is presented as a representation of everyday life. A frontloading leader does not simply say "The lesson I want you to learn today is...," but instead tells participants, "We are going to climb Mount Washington today because the mountain represents...," or "We are going to learn basic canoe skills and paddle the backwaters of the Mississippi River because paddling down the mighty Mississippi is very much like...." With the explicit connection between the educational experience and everyday life, transference of the intended lessons takes place right from the very beginning.

For example, the goal for a group of boys living in a group home might be to improve the group's ability to support each other when unexpected things occur. To address this goal, two staff members take a half dozen boys on a camping trip. Before camp is set up, Dave, one of the trip leaders, sits the group down for a talk:

> *I want you to have fun on this trip, but more importantly, I want you to address a problem that exists back at the center. That problem is that you guys don't support each other. You know this without my having to tell you. Most of you freak out whenever something out of the ordinary happens. When a person makes a mistake, it doesn't occur to anyone to help him correct the mistake. Instead, you jump on the guy's case and accuse him of wrecking everything.*

> *Most of you haven't camped before, so lots of unexpected things are going to happen while we are in the woods. Each of you is going to make mistakes, many more than you usually make back at the center. If we react to those mistakes in our usual way, this trip is going to be a mess. So here's your challenge. I want you to rise above the mistakes. I want you to see mistakes as opportunities to get better. I*

want you to think twice before criticizing someone for goofing up. For the next 4 days, this camp is home—just like the center sometimes is home—just like being back with your parents is home. But there is a difference, and that difference is a clean slate. No bad history with your folks, no bad history with roommates or staff at the center. This is a new place where each of us is a beginner. So when somebody screws up, think about how you react back at the center, and think about how that reaction usually makes things worse.

Being here in nature is great. It's my favorite place to be. But nature also is a place where people have to take responsibility for themselves. If we mess up here, there's no one to bail us out. If we pitch a tent in a bad place, we get wet when it rains. If we wander off by ourselves, we get lost. If we leave the food lying around and the raccoons steal it, no one's driving to town to buy more food. We go without food. Guys, we have consequences here. That's why we came. You guys are ready to handle the challenge—I wouldn't have brought you out here if I thought you weren't ready—but I need each of you to step up.

Obviously, the leaders do not expect that a didactic speech will get the boys to behave responsibly on the camping trip. It is, in fact, a setup. The assumption is that the boys will act on the camping trip the same way as they do at the group home, but that the frontloading will make misbehavior obvious to everyone when it occurs. When the assigned breakfast cook burns the eggs (as will likely happen) and everyone jumps down his throat, the trip leader will not have to tell the group that criticizing the cook is inappropriate behavior. Everyone in the group realizes, "Oh man, this is exactly how we get ourselves in trouble back at the center! This is exactly what Dave was talking about on the first day." When this realization occurs, the camping trip is no longer an end unto itself. It is a metaphor. It is a microcosm of everyday life.

It may be pointing out the obvious, but it is worth mentioning that frontloading makes sense only when the facilitator knows beforehand what the group needs to work on. This means conducting an assessment of the group. A metaphor addresses a specific issue or topic, but a leader must first figure out whether that issue or topic is teamwork or independence, self-confidence or humility, initiative or relaxation, trust or self-reliance, etc.

Dressing the Metaphor

With Facilitator Frontloading, it is not enough to simply frontload the experience and trust that the metaphor will connect with every person in the group. In the words of Stephen Bacon, author of *The Conscious Use of Metaphor*, the metaphor needs to be "dressed."[1] Dressing the metaphor means that the facilitator takes every opportunity to maximize the connections between the metaphor and the real-life issue that the educational experience is intended to represent. The more ways and more times that a metaphor is linked to everyday life, the more effective it will be. This is not as easy as it seems, especially since the activity often is determined before the needs of the group have been identified. In other words, the activity gets chosen before the specific goals and objectives are established; this is contrary to proper curriculum development, but the truth nonetheless. For example, various groups contract with a ropes course before the needs of the groups are clearly defined. And even though these needs will vary, every group goes through the same basic elements on the course. With each group, the belay techniques are the same; the instructions for the various initiatives remain much the same. But because the reasons that these groups come to the ropes course are different, the dressing of the metaphor must be different. The metaphor for a group of corporate executives working on independent thinking is going to have to be different from the metaphor for the women's university volleyball team working on teamwork, just as it is going to have to be different for the teenagers from the local juvenile detention center working on socially appropriate outlets for aggressive behavior.

There are several ways to dress a metaphor. The most direct is simply to stop the action and explicitly make the connection for the group. Facilitators usually notice teachable moments well before any of the participants do, so a facilitator can intercede and remind participants of the original goals and objectives. For example, he might say, "Okay, everybody stop what you are doing for a minute. Twenty minutes ago we said that this spider web activity symbolized mutual trust. Are folks trusting each other right now?"

It is not always necessary to be so direct as to stop the action in order to bring home a point. When a facilitator sees a moment when the metaphoric connection is strong, it might be enough to use short exclamations or non-verbal cues to clue in the participants. For example, a "Yeah!" in conjunction with a big smile will tell a group that something good, maybe a breakthrough by the group, has just occurred.

Stories and story lines might be the most common way to dress a metaphor. Facilitators can compile a collection of fables and entertaining first-person accounts that all have various morals to them. Then during breaks or during setups for the action component of an experience, these stories can be told to make a point. There are, in fact, organizations, that develop entire curricula laced with such stories. The stories become the foundation upon which the activities are built; the activities are designed to match the stories, not the other way around. The Leopold Education Project, for example, developed an environmental education program in which every activity is based on a passage from Aldo Leopold's environmental classic, *A Sand County Almanac*.[2] A more common example is the many religious organizations that have summer camps and other youth ministries where each recreational activity is linked to an important parable or historical event in that religion's teachings. It is easy to imagine adolescents relating better to Moses in the wilderness while on a backpacking trip than while sitting in the basement of a church or synagogue.

Of course stories can come from the participants just as well as the facilitators. As one or two participants start to identify with the metaphor, they may have stories and comments that might make a connection for the others. If their stories come from the very setting that a metaphor is trying to emulate, one participant's story could be the trigger that helps everyone else relate to the metaphor. For example, a group of coworkers are taken on a night hike to point out that they can do things together that they might not do on their own, and the event reminds one of the people in the group of the time they all agreed to work until two in the morning to finish a project back at the office.

And a Final Chance to Make a Point

Theoretically, Facilitator Frontloading makes post-action processing unnecessary. If the facilitator effectively sets up the metaphor *before the action* begins, AND if participants continually link the metaphor to everyday life *during the action*, then formal processing *after the action* is redundant. The lessons of the day should have already taken hold.

Still, most facilitators who frontload also process after the action component of an experience. Because FF is supposed to be unambiguous, facilitators usually do not want to give up one last chance to make an important point. Some even forego a question and answer session and instead bring closure to the program with a speech or closing story. They take full control of the final processing session and explicitly reiterate the purposes of the activity and the meaning of the metaphor. Subtlety might be a strength when the metaphor is from literature or the visual arts, but not so with experiential education. Subtlety in processing is saved for Participant-Directed Processing and Independent Reflection. FF is explicit, used when it is vitally important that everyone appreciates the predetermined outcomes. In FF, the participants get the point in the introduction, they get it during the action, and as often as not, they get it again during some kind of post-activity processing. No one leaves the experience without knowing what it is that they were supposed to learn. No one leaves the experience with the idea, "Gee, I had fun, but I don't really know why we were doing this."

The Participant-Generated Metaphor

The strongest metaphor is the one just described, where the entire educational experience is the metaphor. When, for example, the events of a backpacking trip or a canoe trip replicate the events in the workplace or group home, this is the ideal. It is one real experience (the canoe trip) superimposed onto another real experience (a day on the job, a day at school, etc.). The connections are numerous and often strong, and while this does not mean that every participant in the experience personally identifies with the metaphor, every participant at least recognizes the metaphor and acknowledges the similarities between the activity and everyday life.

Sometimes such all-encompassing metaphors are not possible. Settings such as rivers and mountains and wilderness backcountry have intrinsic meaning, so their impact as metaphors is unique. This does not mean, however, that FF cannot be used in less dramatic settings, e.g., a high school gymnasium or corporate conference room. It just means that the metaphor is not obvious and has to be generated by the facilitator or the participants, then maintained by the group throughout the experience.

A chosen group name is this kind of metaphor. For example, a local juvenile detention center has contracted to use a ropes course one afternoon a week for 8 weeks. On the first day, a dozen teenagers arrive on the course, and the facilitator asks the group to pick a group name. She tells the adolescents that choosing the name must be taken seriously, and the name must represent the way the group will behave while on the course. The group picks the name "Eagles." While the eagle is a bit of a cliché, it also has strong symbolism. The facilitator responds, "Okay, you're the eagles. What does an eagle represent?" The group comes up with terms like bravery, independence, vigilance, and dignity. Early in the sessions, the facilitator frequently asks if the group is living up to the eagle name. In the second session, she gives each participant an army surplus shoulder patch with an eagle embroidered on it. Before long, the kids develop the mantra, "Be an eagle!" If a participant becomes discouraged when she makes a mistake during an initiative, the others tell her to be as confident as an eagle. When a second participant needs encouragement to climb onto a high element of the ropes course, the other kids tell him to soar like an eagle.

Yangtze's River: An Example of Dressing the Metaphor

In the conversation between McKinley and Yangtze, Yangtze suggested the intriguing metaphor of processing being like a river. What if she wanted to put that metaphor to work? What if she held a staff training at her university outdoor center about the importance of processing?

Yangtze recognizes that her staff members are familiar with several processing techniques, but seldom process the groups that they work with. The staff effectively teaches outdoor skills such as kayaking, sailing, and rock climbing, but they almost never process as part of the teaching. Students sign up for outdoor center offerings to learn technical skills, so most of her facilitators focus entirely on teaching these skills. Therefore, Yangtze chooses, as the topic of one of their monthly training sessions, the importance of processing. She organizes a one-day canoe and kayak trip on a nearby river. The trip will show the staff a section of river most are not familiar with, but the explicit purpose of the training is processing. What can Yangtze do to dress the metaphor?

First, she must fully define the metaphor for herself. What specifically did she mean when she said that processing is like a river? Rivers are symbolic of many things, but how can these symbols effectively be linked to processing and reflection? Before the training session, Yangtze clarifies the metaphor. She comes up with the following list:

1. All water, rivers included, can reflect like a mirror. Processing is reflection, an attempt to recapture the major events of an experience.

2. Water, rivers included, is the source of life for all things on the planet. Plants and animals drink from the river directly; some predators prey upon animals that live in the water. Processing satisfies a thirst as well: the desire to put meaning to events.

3. Rivers seldom change overnight. Instead, they slowly undercut banks until the banks collapse under their own weight. Over time an entirely new watercourse might be created. Processing can cut away at an old way of thinking and start a group of participants upon a new path.

4. Rivers flood. Floods destroy, but they also bring water and nutrients to parched areas. They create new channels. Processing is a way to wash away misconceptions and create new channels of thinking.

5. There is a truism that a person cannot step in the same river twice. This is, in itself, a metaphor to suggest that no two experiences in life have the exact same lessons to teach.

6. Rivers are a key component of the water cycle, just as processing is a key component of the experiential education cycle.

7. In spite of their great power, rivers seek the path of least resistance; rivers go with the flow. Processing helps people to go with the flow. It helps them to identify the right path, often a path that is going with the flow.

8. Huckleberry Finn's adventure on the Mississippi River is a lesson in non-conformity, individuality, and freedom. This is an important concept, because going with the flow does not necessarily mean following the masses. It is finding the path that is best for the individual, and finding such a path requires reflection.

9. Rivers begin as trickles, then grow, and eventually empty into a lake, a sea, or an ocean. Concepts brought to

light through processing may begin small, then grow, then flow into a person's overall image of the world.

With a clearer image of the metaphor in mind, Yangtze is ready for the outing. She wants to frontload the experience, but because the entry spot is along a busy highway, she first has the group paddle for 20 minutes before beaching the canoes and kayaks on a small sandbar. She has everyone gather into a small circle on the sand. Then, she says:

> I know that I told you that the purpose of this month's staff training was processing, but I never really told you why the session was being conducted on a river. The reason is this: Those of you who have been working at the center for a year or more have been exposed to at least a half dozen process- ing techniques. We've gone through several question and answer sessions, plus we've used processing cards and talk- ing sticks and some other processing tools. I also gave each of you a small journal when I hired you, so those of you who regularly write in your journals know that journaling is a way of reflecting. Still, we run a lot of programs through the center where no processing occurs. And, to be honest, I'd like to see more processing in our offerings.

> I'll take most of the blame for the lack of processing. The monthly training sessions stress technical skills over pro- cessing techniques. My own processing style might seem haphazard, so it comes across that I don't think processing is important. But just because I don't finish each session with a processing activity does not mean that processing is unimportant. Today I want to show all of you how I think about processing. To me, processing is like a river.

> How many of you have heard of the Wild and Scenic Rivers Act? About half of you? The Wild and Scenic Rivers Act is a federal law that says some rivers shouldn't have dams and shouldn't have cabins and resorts and other man-made structures up and down the banks. This law insures that at least some rivers stay natural. But the reason for Wild and Scenic Rivers isn't to protect nature. It's not to have a

nice place for birds and fish and bears and deer. Wild and Scenic Rivers are for people. They are places for people to slow down, relax, and reflect. Even politicians, people who I do not think of as being particularly reflective, have recognized that one of the best places for people to slow down and reflect is on a river. I don't need to tell most of you this. You kayak or canoe for recreation and know from personal experience that rivers put you into a reflective mood. A few hours on the river, and most of you instinctively relax and almost unconsciously start to reflect on deeper things. Because rivers have this effect, I think processing is like a river in that it is a way to get people to slow down and reflect. It is a way to get people to sift through the jumble that is their lives and distinguish which aspects are important. So before you start wondering what kind of tangent I am off on, please listen for just a minute or two.

Today we are going to paddle a section of the Black River. I picked this stretch because it has some fun Class II rapids on it. Between the rapids are quarter-mile sections of gently flowing flat water. Today I want you to do something for me. While we are in those quiet sections, I want you to make an effort to be more reflective than usual. Try not to talk to each other about stuff that has nothing to do with the river, stuff like school or movies or boyfriend/girlfriend problems. Don't start splashing each other and goofing around. Instead, notice the fluidity of your canoe stroke, the beauty of the water, the plants and animals on the banks. I'm not expecting you to turn into river monks, but I am asking you to be aware of your surroundings. Most experiential education is action followed by reflection followed by action followed by reflection. The river is exactly the same. Rapids followed by quiet stretches followed by rapids followed by quiet stretches. During the rapids, none of you will be doing much reflecting. You will be focused on the challenge of getting through the rapids without dumping or getting caught on a rock. While in the rapids, the water and the paddling will have your complete attention. Then there will be stretches of quiet water where you can relax. The quiet water is the reflection, the opportunity to let your mind wander a bit and maybe come across something profound. During these quiet stretches, you naturally slip into a meditative state, a condition that you can hold until you hear or see the next set of rapids and again gear up for some action.

The point I want to make is that you need and should welcome the quiet stretches. All action and no reflection is experience out of balance. Throughout the day, we may occasionally pull ashore to formally process, but that is not the important part of today's in-service. I don't care whether you notice the processing techniques that I use today. The important part is for you to get into the rhythm of the river, because I want you to consider whether the action-reflection of the river is a pattern you might want to emulate in your teaching.

Yangtze has planted the metaphor, and the paddlers return to the river. Occasional water fights still break out. Participants don't spend every minute of the day reflecting on how processing is like a river, but just as Yangtze told the group, the river creates reflective states of mind. Because of Yangtze's front-loading, paddlers notice the rhythm of the river and appreciate it a bit more than they otherwise would.

Throughout the trip, Yangtze takes opportunities to dress the metaphor. As with all canoe trips, the paddlers get spread out along the river, so she cannot talk to everyone at the same time. That does not matter. Whenever a teachable moment presents itself, she conveys it to whomever is within earshot. With one canoe, she says, "Look at the heron over there. It stands completely still, silent and still, yet is aware of all things. I am sure that it knows where we are, yet if a fish or frog passes in front of its feet, it moves instantly and grabs its prey in its beak. I doubt it is thinking back on that great leopard frog that it snagged yesterday. Instead its mind is completely open to all that is happening now."

Twenty minutes later Yangtze pulls up alongside another canoe and tries to make the same point using a completely different image. She says, "Look at the reflection of those maple trees in the water. It captures the beauty of the trees so perfectly that if I took a photograph of the scene and showed the photo to a friend, she'd have a hard time telling which image was the trees and which was the reflection of the trees in the water. The river reflects a moment in perfect detail."

Again and again, one boat at a time, she points out aspects of the river that represent peacefulness, quiet, and reflection. It might be an eddy, an expanding ripple caused by a surfacing fish, even the little whirlpools made with each paddle stroke.

For lunch, the group pulls onto a sandbar to eat sandwiches. While eating, Yangtze tells them about her first time on a river. She says:

> Believe it or not, the first time I ever paddled in whitewater was in a race. I was 16 years old, and my new boyfriend was a whitewater racer. He did slalom racing, where canoe and kayak paddlers maneuvered their boats through gates up and down the river. I went with him to a race, and after we got there, he conned me into entering a race called C2-mixed. The C was for canoe, 2 was for two people, and mixed meant one male and one female. The course was impossible; some gates required paddling upstream and others required ferrying across the river. I didn't know anything—but ladies, he was Brad Pitt before there was a Brad Pitt, and I was young and stupid. I would have followed him anywhere, and so I did. He said that he'd teach me two strokes, put me in the bow, and we'd be fine. The two strokes he taught me were the draw and the sweep. One stroke to help the boat go left, and one stroke to help the boat go right.
>
> The course was set up through a series of rapids just up- stream from a small waterfall. There were probably 30 yards between the finish line and the waterfall, so any

skilled paddler could easily get to shore without going over the falls. You can guess what happened. We ran the course, and after passing through the last gate, my dream boat of a boyfriend yelled, "Draw, draw!" to help us get to shore. I was scared silly, so I did exactly the opposite. The louder he yelled draw, the harder I swept, and we went right over the waterfall. We dumped; I freaked. I let go of my paddle, and it drifted downstream. My boyfriend momentarily got caught in the turbulence, and he lost contact with the canoe—so it headed down the river, too. Rescue boats below the waterfall shot out from both banks. As soon as they realized that both of us were safe, they paddled downstream to retrieve the lost equipment.

My boyfriend said, "Well, that could have gone better," but he said it with this big grin that told me he was having the time of his life. I wanted to punch him in the nose, but instead I dragged myself out of the river looking like a wet dog. I was really mad, and as nice as he tried to be, I wasn't going to let him off the hook for scaring me and making me look like a fool. That night, however, people sat around the campfire and talked about the day. Of course, our fiasco at the waterfall was a main topic of conversation. My boyfriend took a lot of kidding—his friends said that he'd finally found a girl who'd go out with him and then he nearly drowned her. With me, however, these people were unbelievably kind—sympathetic without being condescending. They said that, except for the major screw-up at the end, I'd done amazingly well—so well that I must have felt "it" at least part of the time. And by "it" they meant the flow of the river. They meant that I must have felt the flow of the river.

Whether they realized it or not, those people around that campfire helped me process the experience. First they acknowledged my fear during parts of the race. Then they helped me realize that I wasn't afraid all of the time. There had been stretches where I focused on the paddling and had a sense of what it meant to be one with the water.

It was during that campfire that I got hooked on paddling. In the months that followed, I had my boyfriend teach me to paddle, then I dumped his good-looking butt—or maybe it was the other way around; I don't remember. But the love of being on the water has stayed with me to this day. Heck, it has me right now as I watch the river flow by.

Let me read a short passage from an essay called The Flow of the River. It's by an anthropologist named Loren Eiseley. He was famous for saying, "If there is magic on this planet, it is contained in water." In this essay, Eiseley was standing in the shallows of the Platte River on the Great Plains studying some plants when he had an uncontrollable urge to become part of the river. So, he laid face up in the river and let it carry him away. He wrote,

> "The notion came to me, I suppose, by degrees. I had shed my clothes and was floundering pleasantly in a hole among some reeds when a great desire to stretch out and go with this gently insistent water began to pluck at me.... I lay back in the floating position that left my face to the sky, and shoved off. The sky wheeled over me. For an instant, as I bobbed into the main channel, I had the sensation of sliding down the vast tilted face of the continent. It was then that I felt the cold needles of alpine springs at my fingertips, and the warmth of the Gulf (of Mexico) pulling me southward. Moving with me, leaving its taste upon my mouth and spouting under me in dancing springs of sand, was the immense body of the continent itself, flowing like the river was flowing, grain by grain, mountain by mountain, down to the sea.... I was water... then I finally edged gently against a sand bar and dropped like any log. I tottered as I rose. I knew once more the body's revolt against emergence into the harsh unsupporting air, its reluctance to break contact with that mother element which still, at this late point in time, shelters and brings into being nine tenths of everything alive."[3]

This great quote puts into words my feelings about rivers better than I can. Being one with the water is being part of everything. As Eiseley said, it is being part of the whole continent moving toward the sea. Although this is a bit of a stretch, this is the kind of thing I'd like to see more in our programs. Now I know that a two-hour workshop on basic canoe strokes is not going to bring anyone to a transcendent experience with the river, but it's a start. It's a first step, and one way to maximize the impact of that first step is to process. Point out that the canoe workshop was more than learning how to draw and sweep. It was creating a connection with the universe. Please just give this some thought.

Yangtze stops talking and lets people finish their lunch. Then the paddlers get back on the river. Yangtze again does a little one-on-one dressing of the metaphor as they paddle down the river. This time, instead of telling people to look at herons and ripples and reflections in the water, she asks individuals whether they have any special stories about their times on water. Finally, about a half mile from the takeout spot, Yangtze takes the group ashore for the last time and gets them into a processing circle. She tells the group, "In a few minutes we'll reach the takeout spot, load up the boats, and head home. Before we do, I want to process a little bit. If the purpose of the day is to stress the importance of processing and reflection, I think that I better set an example and do a little formal processing. I am hoping that you've been thinking all day about the flow of rivers and the flow of reflective thinking. That's because there is, as Eiseley said, magic in water. It's also because most of American history is about humanity's connection with nature. Some of that history is ugly, with senseless destruction of nature and indigenous peoples, but some of it is also beautiful and romantic. I have only one question for you, 'Will this paddling trip cause you to process more in your own programs?' Answer honestly. If you will process more, explain why. If you probably won't process anymore than you do already, tell us why the metaphor of the river as processing does not move you to process more with your groups."

Conclusion

Of course, Yangtze's use of the river is not an original idea. The river is one of the most powerful of all metaphors. Entire literary works (*Heart of Darkness, Huckleberry Finn, A River Runs Through It, Big Two-Hearted River, The Concord and the Merrimac*) rely on the river to carry a theme. The trip by Yangtze was only a taste of what the river metaphor can be. Other settings, however, also have this kind of potential. Mountains, lakes, cityscapes, and coastlines all carry strong symbolism. A worthwhile exercise is to look at your own work setting and identify the symbolism associated with it. From that symbolism comes the material for dressing the metaphor and implementing Facilitator Frontloading.

The Standard: Developing Better Questions and Answers

Processing is like slow-pitch softball.
The pitches are lobbed so everyone can play,
but that doesn't necessarily make the game easy.

The most common and arguably the most reliable method of processing is a question and answer session conducted immediately after the action portion of the learning experience. For some experiential educators, it is the only way that they process—and if they do it well, sticking with the tried and true is not a bad way to go. Question and answer (aka Outward Bound Plus) has many positive attributes. For example:

- Q & A allows the facilitator to control the processing topics and simultaneously involve participants at a fairly high level.

- Q & A can be prepared during the planning stages of an event, but is flexible enough to be changed on the spot if necessary.

- Q & A has a high chance of success, meaning that a competent questioner should almost always be able to convey worthwhile ideas through his or her choice of questions.

One reason question and answer sessions are effective is because both facilitators and participants are actively involved. The facilitators can control the direction of the discussion by carefully sequencing questions, and at the same time, they can relinquish parcels of that control either by stepping back

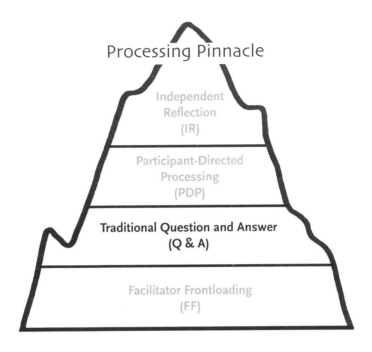

Processing Pinnacle

Independent
Reflection
(IR)

Participant-Directed
Processing
(PDP)

**Traditional Question and Answer
(Q & A)**

Facilitator Frontloading
(FF)

from the conversation when it takes off on its own or by asking follow-up questions that directly relate to topics initiated by the participants. The ability to regulate the level of participant autonomy is appealing to many leaders. In fact, it borders on the ideal, because it is granting freedom to participants without giving up much authority. If a discussion takes off in a productive direction, the leader sits back, and the participants experience the joy of self-processing. If the discussion digresses into meaningless anecdotes or non-productive bickering, the leader can gently step in and say, "I'd like to take the discussion in a slightly different direction by asking...."

Traditional Question and Answer is the happy medium of processing. For the average group, Q & A offers the appropriate mix of facilitator and participant input. For the experienced group that is capable of process on its own, it is not so prescriptive as to be insulting. For the group that needs to be taken by the hand at every turn, it guides facilitator-dependent participants toward useful insights and conclusions. Q & A is not the best processing technique for every situation, but it almost always is a safe and dependable option.

If we see question and answer as the mainstay of processing, all experiential educators should continually work on their skills in facilitating question and answer sessions. The following are a few suggestions for making incremental improvements to Q & A.

Welcome Silence

The simplest word of advice about improving question and answer sessions is to allow for periods of silence between the time a question is asked and the time participants respond. Clifford Knapp calls this "wait time."[1] Facilitators can wait out the participants when they begin to fidget, look down at their feet, and poke the ground with a stick. Facilitators should not intentionally make processing uncomfortable, but neither should they bail out participants when the participants avoid the responsibility of reflecting on an experience and expressing their views. Most educators do not give students enough time to think about the question being asked. In the absence of a response, they jump in and fill in the dead space. Sometimes facilitators will rephrase the question, but often as not, they just answer the question themselves. If the question is at all thought provoking, a few seconds is not enough time for anyone to consider the question and come up with an intelligent response. It is enough time, however, for people to begin to feel uncomfortable with the silence. This applies to facilitators as much as it does participants, so the tendency is for facilitators to speak up when the participants do not. If facilitators go into a question and answer session expecting periods of silence, they can easily sit quietly while participants weigh questions, formulate answers, and garner the courage to speak up.

Listen Carefully

A companion skill to welcoming silence is listening well. There are actually two periods of silence during a processing session. The first, as was just discussed, is the time between a question being asked and a question being answered. The second period of silence is the time between participants answering one question and a facilitator asking a follow-up question. This is another interval when facilitators should learn to accept momentary quiet. The natural tendency of most people is to listen to the first few words of what a person is saying, then tune that person out and begin to formulate a response or a follow-up question. For example, have you ever been asked a two-part question in a job interview, and halfway through an answer, had to ask, "I'm sorry. What was the second part of the question?" You heard the first part of the question, then disregarded the second part while you thought about a response to the first part. The processing equivalent of this habit is for a facilitator to formulate a follow-up question before the participants have finished talking. In other words, the facilitator is thinking about question two while the group is still talking about question one. The facilitator wants question two ready to go as soon as there is a break in the discussion, but in preparing for that question, he or she has stopped listening to all that is being said. A facilitator needs to unlearn any tendencies to fast forward during processing sessions and then listen to the full statements of the people answering questions. This might mean that the group must sit through a few seconds of silence while the facilitator formulates a follow-up question, but that question will be based upon the full conversation, not just the first sentence or two. One way that some facilitators address this problem is to have a small pad of paper during processing. Any time a good follow-up question comes to mind, the facilitator can quickly write down a keyword and immediately get back to the conversation. When the participants are finished talking, the facilitator can glance at the keyword and recall the follow-up question.

Develop Two Sets of Questions

A facilitator conducting Q & A often has two sets of questions. The first set is the questions that were written during initial planning and relate to the predetermined goals and objectives. The second set is what the facilitator spontaneously generates when something unexpected occurs during the action component of an experience. For example, the goal of the day may be cooperation and team building, so a facilitator, well before the group shows up, writes a half dozen questions about cooperation and team building. However, when an otherwise responsible group ignores the rules of safety during a particular group initiative, the facilitator stops the action for fear that someone will get hurt. He restates the rules, demands that the rules be followed, and allows the group to finish. He also, on the spot, jots down a handful of questions about the incident. When the post-activity processing session takes place, questions of safety supersede the originally planned topic.

Cofacilitate Whenever Possible

There is a big difference between cofacilitating a program and working it as a tag team. Facilitators who tag team take turns. One facilitator leads an activity, and a second facilitator is off somewhere else getting another activity ready. Facilitator One leads the group through the first activity, processes that activity, then hands the group over to Facilitator Two. While the second activity is taking place, the first facilitator uses a few minutes to catch her breath, then starts setting up activity number three. The two leaders might work together at the very beginning of the session and again at the very end, but for the most part, they are taking turns. This style of facilitation gives leaders valuable downtime, but it also means that the two leaders seldom interact with the group at the same time.

An alternate approach is true cofacilitation, meaning both facilitators are involved in all activities. Very often one leader oversees the action, and the other assumes responsibility for the processing. The facilitator doing the processing can simply watch the action and be on the lookout for teachable moments. He may occasionally stop the action to discuss something with a group, but more often he is quietly making observations that will be turned into questions for the processing session. The "action" facilitator can focus entirely on the immediate needs of the group, not worrying about teachable moments and post-action processing. The "processing" facilitator can focus entirely on processing, making observations and writing well-worded questions.

Luckner and Nadler, in their book *Processing the Experience*, point out that teachable moments do not exist in a vacuum.[2]

There are revealing occurrences that lead up to the teachable moment, and there are observable changes after the moment. These kinds of things can be subtle and may go unnoticed by people immersed in the action—and unfortunately, a facilitator working solo can be just as immersed in the action as the participants. It is not fair to expect one person to focus on the immediate needs of a group and simultaneously watch for the nuances of an experience. With two facilitators working together, however, one leader can dedicate her full attention to the present action, while a second leader can observe the action, analyze significant turning points, and transform his observations into engaging processing questions. Usually the reason for on-the-spot processing is not to point out that a group had a breakthrough; that, as often as not, is obvious. Rather it is 1) to discover what happened beforehand to allow for the breakthrough and 2) to discuss what is different now that the breakthrough has occurred.

Ask Questions in an Appropriate Order

One of the small classics of processing literature is a short article by Quinsland and Van Ginkel titled "How to Process Experience."[3] Quinsland and Van Ginkel offer a quick, straightforward technique for putting processing questions in an appropriate order. While we recommend that you track down the article for yourself, the premise of the piece is that a significant impediment to effective Q & A is asking difficult questions too early in a session. For example, a common opening question sometimes is, "So how did you feel about the last activity?" Although determining feelings is a reasonable goal for processing, this is a poor first question. First of all, "how do you feel" is inexact. Without the proper setup, participants do not know what the question means. Second, participants need a certain level of comfort before they will express their feelings honestly. Asking them a feeling question at the beginning of a processing session is just as likely to put a group on its guard as it is to get them to open up. A suit-and-tie corporate group required to go on a ropes course might already have an image of ropes courses as touchy-feely mumbo jumbo, and starting them off with a feelings question will confirm this perception. Feeling questions need to be set up with easier, more straightforward questions.

Quinsland and Van Ginkel offer a three-step approach for sequencing questions. Step One is to write down the most important questions to be asked, not worrying initially about the order in which they will be asked.

Step Two is to determine the level of difficulty of these important questions. The way that Quinsland and Van Ginkel did this was to match the questions with the various levels of Bloom's taxonomy. Bloom's taxonomy is a model that breaks cognition or thinking into six progressively more sophisticated levels. The levels are

1) knowledge (memorization),
2) comprehension (ability to explain knowledge in a literal way),
3) application (ability to use knowledge to solve rote problems),
4) analysis (ability to break knowledge into its component parts),
5) synthesis (ability to put the pieces back together to create a whole), and
6) evaluation (ability to make informed judgments and opinions).

Step Three is organizing questions into a sequence where the easiest questions get asked first, and progressively more difficult questions follow. If all of the important questions are fairly difficult, the facilitator should add a few easy questions to flesh out the sequence.

Quinsland and Van Ginkel's three-step process remains popular in experiential education, although many facilitators do not use Bloom's taxonomy as the measure of the difficulty of their questions. Instead they use a taxonomy of their own making, with levels that might include fact-finding questions, analysis and synthesis questions, feelings questions, and transference questions.[4]

Ask Worthwhile Questions

Facilitators should avoid redundant and pointless questions. While this seems obvious, experiential educators sometimes reach a point in a program when it feels like a good time to process, but they have nothing of substance to talk about. Maybe the goals of the event were never clearly delineated, and there are no predetermined questions to ask. The facilitator assumed that the events of the day would generate some interesting questions, but nothing eventful has occurred during the first few activities. Now it is time to reflect, and the facilitator has nothing that he really wants to discuss. Feeling obligated to have a question and answer session, he throws out a couple of stock questions and, to no one's surprise, gets a handful of cliché responses. Both the facilitator and the participants go through the motions of processing.

While no real harm is done by asking poor questions, it does substantiate some people's perception that processing is the boring downtime between interesting activities. When there is nothing worthwhile to talk about, facilitators should 1) not process just for the sake of processing, 2) do a better job planning for the next group, so there is something to talk about, and 3) consider whether they were not paying close enough attention during the action component, perhaps missing topics worthy of discussion.

Customize Questions for Specific Audiences

Some facilitators customize questions for every single group. This is excellent detail for those with the time and talent to tweak the questions for every group that goes through a program. Other facilitators customize questions for each kind of audience (e.g., corporate groups, sports teams) that utilizes a program, and this is a bare minimum. Themes may be the same, but the tenor of the questions must vary depending on the kind of group.

Appendix B of this book consists of a list of over 200 processing questions. While the questions are organized according to theme, they are, out of necessity, generic when it comes to audience. In most cases, a facilitator would not use these questions exactly as they appear on the page, but would reword them slightly to fit the group that will be answering the question. For example, one question in the list is "How was trust for this activity any different from the trust that occurs on a day-to-day basis?" This question lacks specificity. A better question (e.g., for a cross-country team) would be "How was the trust that you showed the spotters during the trust fall any different from the trust that you show each other when your team is in the middle of a race?" Another better question (e.g., for an alcohol treatment group) would be "Why do you trust each other with your physical safety on the trust fall, but show little trust when you meet each week for group therapy?"

Fine-Tune the Wording of Your Questions

A facilitator should be comfortable with asking questions off the cuff and not be worried about exact wording, but at the same time there is no reason why the prepared questions should not be carefully worded. Three easy checks are as follows:

✓ CHECK No. 1: THE YES/NO TEST. As much as possible, a facilitator should avoid questions that can be answered with only a word or two. If a question can be answered with either "yes" or "no," the facilitator should find ways to bridge the subject in a different way. For example, "Has this canoe trip brought you closer to nature?" is not a well-constructed question. It gives respondents a chance to simply answer "yes" or "no." Obviously, a facilitator can always ask a respondent to elaborate on a one-word answer, but a better question is "What, if anything, has brought you closer to nature on this trip?" Also better is "Please describe specific examples on this trip when you felt a personal connection with the natural world." If processing were an examination, it would be an essay exam, not a true/false quiz.

✓ CHECK No. 2: THE JARGON TEST. Jargon is a double-edged sword. If facilitators know the jargon of a particular group, incorporating it into a question and answer session will personalize the processing. Conversely, if facilitators pepper Q & A with jargon that makes no sense to a group, they not only mess up the processing session, but also create a distinction between themselves and the group. Experiential educators should be especially aware of the jargon of experiential education. It's easy to forget that everyone does not use the terminology of one's own profession. "Facilitator" is jargon for a teacher or a leader. "Processing" is jargon for talking about what just happened. "Moving out of our comfort zone" is jargon for doing something that is physically or emotionally unsettling.

✓ CHECK NO. 3: THE BIAS TEST. The most difficult check of the three is the bias test. This involves evaluating questions to determine whether they express the facilitators' opinions and/or push respondents to answer one way over another. In some instances, the bias is obvious and can be easily corrected. For example, the question "After spending a week in the backcountry, why do you think wilderness is better than suburbia?" is biased. A better question that makes the same point is "After spending a week backpacking, what differences do you see between wilderness and suburbia?" Participants still will extol the virtues of wilderness, but this version of the question leaves the door open for the facilitator to ask, "But what things about your suburban lifestyle are you going to miss if we stay out in the backcountry much longer?"

Some processing questions can be biased without being blatantly so. For example, the question "What can we do to lessen conflict?" is a reasonable question to ask a group that is not working together, but it implicitly suggests that conflict is bad and cooperation/compromise is good. In the same manner, the question "What steps should we take to plan better?" is a well-intentioned question designed to encourage a group to discuss strategy before charging into a project, but it can also be a criticism of spontaneous action. If a group does not get along, then questions about reducing conflict make sense. Also, groups that repeatedly jump into action without planning will benefit with processing questions that encourage pre-planning. It is important, however, for facilitators to remember that conflict and spontaneous action have as much place in experiential education as cooperation and planning.

Serve as Gatekeeper

Facilitators who conduct a question and answer session are more than a generator of questions. They are also gatekeepers. A facilitator has the authority to choose who talks. Facilitators need to control people who dominate the conversation, talk over others, and cut others off in mid-sentence. Facilitators need to keep the conversation on point. They need to draw out people who are reticent to speak. Part of this responsibility is setting ground rules for the Q & A. The other part is making sure that the ground rules are followed.

Conclusion

When experiential educators say "Processing is difficult," many of them really mean "Q & A is difficult." It is public speaking, thinking on one's feet, and managing group dynamics—all rolled up into a single task. Still it is hard to imagine good processing without competently led question and answer sessions. Even with all of the new and clever processing techniques being developed and used in the last several years, good processing is built around the ability to ask worthwhile questions and garner thoughtful answers. Observing other processors may be a helpful introduction to developing Q & A skills, but eventually the only way to facilitate Q & A effectively is to dive in and do it. The tips listed above may help a facilitator tune his or her skills, but leading discussions with confidence only comes with practice.

Participant-Directed Processing

> Processing is like ice cream. Any flavor of ice cream is
> better than no ice cream at all. Question and answer sessions
> are the vanilla of processing, the dependable standard and the
> base from which all other flavors flow. As good as vanilla is,
> most facilitators can't help but try new flavors. Sometimes
> these taste tests lead to a magical blend of chocolate chips and
> cookie dough; other times the facilitator is left with two scoops
> of garlic ice cream on a stale wafer cone.

Question and answer sessions are basic experiential education.
Because most people have been schooled in traditional education, this straightforward approach to processing works well
with people not versed in untraditional methodologies. With Q
& A, the facilitator can keep the themes fairly basic and gently
guide participants to a few useful conclusions. Participants,
even if they have not been trained in facilitated processing, will
participate in a question and answer session and recognize the
usefulness of verbally analyzing an activity just completed.

As participants have more and more opportunities to be involved in experiential education, however, the options for processing expand. Over time, those active in experiential education fall into the rhythms of this alternative style of learning,
and they come to appreciate the value of reflection.* When this
happens, processing that initially focused on the predetermined
outcomes can move in new directions, and one of the best new

---

* An excellent example of this phenomenon is a group of professional
experiential educators at an experiential education workshop. As soon
as there is a lull in the action, these experienced facilitators break into
spontaneous processing. When these same educators fill out evaluations
at the end of the workshop, a common comment might be, "The content
was good, but we didn't get enough time to process."

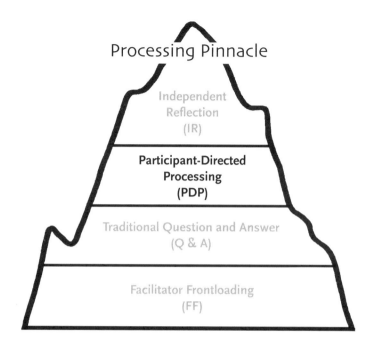

Processing Pinnacle

Independent
Reflection
(IR)

**Participant-Directed
Processing
(PDP)**

Traditional Question and Answer
(Q & A)

Facilitator Frontloading
(FF)

directions is teaching participants the skills to process on their own. As the reasons for processing change, so too might the processing methodologies. In fact, the underlying principle of the Processing Pinnacle is that *processing methodologies change as the reasons for processing change.*

Participant-Directed Processing Revisited

Chapter 5 of this book briefly defined Participant-Directed Processing. Now is a good time to elaborate on that definition. PDP is a collection of processing techniques whereby a facilitator requires a formal processing session, even chooses the processing technique, but asks the participants to assume primary responsibility for the direction of the reflection. The methodology shows the participants how to process, but does not walk them through the processing session itself. The participants, usually as a group, do this extensively on their own. The facilitator consciously eases up on the processing reins and turns some of the responsibility for the success of the processing over to the participants. PDP, at its best, provides participants with a way to process and shows them that they can process on their own. A basic tenet of experiential education is for the facilitator to fade into the background when a group is able to handle a task on its own. PDP is applying this basic tenet to processing.

A good example of PDP is time set aside for journaling. So long as the facilitator is not prescriptive about the content of the journal entries, participants are required to reflect, but are able to take that reflection in any direction. If the participants then re-group to read journal excerpts to each other, the exercise is also a lesson in the varied potential of journaling as a reflective tool. In the same way, dyads (breaking a large group into pairs or trios and allowing them to reflect in small groups) also show participants that they are capable of processing without help from the facilitator. If the dyads come back together and each dyad summarizes its discussion for the larger group, everyone can see that processing may go off in several different directions and still be worthwhile. Dyads, along with concept maps and processing cards, are PDP techniques described in detail in appendix A.

Obviously, relinquishing full control of the processing has a downside. Order and efficiency are compromised. There is the chance that predetermined outcomes do not get discussed. When a facilitator gives up these things, it is fair to expect something in return. Some of the possible benefits of PDP include:

- PARTICIPANTS MAY COME UP WITH THE PREDETERMINED OUTCOMES ON THEIR OWN. Passing responsibility for the content of the processing on to the participants does not necessarily mean that the program's predetermined goals and objectives get overlooked. A group that has gone through a number of question and answer sessions, and has experienced examples of frontloading, will know that a primary purpose of processing is to bring out the lessons of an experience. Free to take processing in any direction they want, it is probable that participants will focus in on the same subjects that the facilitator would have. There will be, however, the added benefit that the group came upon these themes without extensive facilitator guidance. The Chinese classic *Tao Te Ching* says that the best leaders are those who lay the groundwork for their followers, yet when the task is complete, the followers say, "Oh, we did it all on our own."[1]

- PARTICIPANTS MOVE PROCESSING INTO UNEXPECTED, BUT USEFUL DIRECTIONS. A group using PDP may process about an activity's predetermined goals and objectives. They also might take the processing in an entirely unexpected direction. When facilitators can give participants the authority to control much of the processing, they are showing comfort with letting the processing go where it may. The facilitators are willing to sacrifice guaranteed results if it enhances participant independence. When facilitators hand responsibility for processing over to the participants, it is not because they think that the participants will always weed out the predetermined goals and objectives on their own. It is because facilitators want the participants to process on their own and are willing to let discussion bypass the predetermined outcomes altogether and center on other subjects. Sometimes the paths taken by the participants will be dead ends. Other times these new directions will open avenues of entirely new insight.

- PARTICIPANTS BEGIN TO SELF-PROCESS. In PDP, facilitators do not direct the processing so much as mentor it. One purpose of PDP is that participants hone their processing skills under the watchful eye of an experienced processor. If all is well within a processing session, the facilitator keeps quiet. If the group struggles, the facilitator can step in and give advice on how to process more effectively. The role of the facilitator shifts from leading the processing session to teaching the group how to reflect on its own. The results of the PDP session may not be as in depth as a facilitator-led session, but it is a step toward self-processing. PDP shows participants that they can begin to process without a facilitator in charge.

The Second Kind of Transference

Transference is learning a skill in one setting with the purpose of applying that same skill somewhere else. For example, a goal of a ropes and challenge course program might be cooperation and team building. Transference, in this case, means that not only did a group cooperate and bond during the time that they were on the ropes course, but it carried that cooperative spirit over to the setting where the group interacts on a daily basis. During a question and answer session about cooperation and team building, a facilitator might broach the subject of transference by asking, "You've told me that at work many of you are at each others' throats. Today, I've seen almost none of that. With a few minor exceptions, all of you have been friendly and cooperative. Why was today different, and what can you do to extend this camaraderie to your daily jobs?"

There is another kind of transference, a more generic form not linked to specific goals and objectives. This second kind of transference involves instilling people with an overall philosophy of learning experientially. In other words, it is making a facilitated experience so positive and educational that it opens the door to other experiences. Dewey calls this second form of transference "an immediate aspect of agreeableness... and its influence upon later experiences."[2]

For example, a woman who signs up for a continuing education course in backyard composting is so taken with the course that she signs up for three more continuing education courses— none of them having anything to do with compost or gardening. The woman went into the class to learn how to turn her lawn clippings into soil, but came out with a strong desire to learn experientially. A paradox of experiential education is that no one signs up for a class or workshop with the express purpose of finding his or her personal philosophy of education, yet instilling a person with such a perspective (i.e., opening the door to a lifetime of experiencing) might be the most worthwhile thing an experiential educator can do.

An important aspect of instilling people with a philosophy of experiential learning is teaching them to process on their own. When experiential educators promote a life of experiencing, they also must teach their students how to reflect on those experiences. Facilitator Frontloading, for all its positive attributes, does not teach people how to process. It bluntly says, "Here! These are the important things to learn, so let's go learn them." Independent Reflection, which is extensively no facilitator guidance at all, also does not do a good job of teaching people how to process on their own. IR works best when participants already know how to process; in fact, it assumes participants know how to process on their own. IR says, "You've had an experience, you know how to process, and your facilitator is trusting that you will process by yourself."

Therefore, in the four levels of the Processing Pinnacle, it falls upon Q & A and PDP to do the actual teaching of processing. Q & A generates the enthusiasm for reflection, and PDP provides instruction on how to reflect. Q & A reveals the potential of effective processing, and PDP shows people that processing is a skill that can be learned.

A Stepping-Stone Approach

When a facilitator is willing to turn responsibility for the success of required processing over to the participants, a few conditions must exist. Most important is that members of the group possess the maturity and skills to process on their own. If a group does not take processing seriously when allowed to process on its own, participants within that group are not ready to self-process. If a group is serious about processing, but has not been through enough processing sessions to appreciate the potential of careful reflection, some members of that group may not have the skills to process on their own. A group not ready to assume responsibility for processing will start the discussion with, "So, what do the facilitators want us to do?" A group that is ready to assume responsibility will not ask or, for that matter, care what the facilitators want; they will dive into the challenge of processing on their own.

Learning to process independently may be analogous to a young girl learning to read. In her pre-school years, Mom or Dad reads to the girl every night before bed (this is comparable to Q & A). Being read to spurs the girl's interest in books, but it is not reading on her own. At age 5 or 6, with the help of her parents and teachers, the girl starts to actually read (this is basic PDP). The books are very simple, not as complicated as the books that the parents were reading to the girl, but it is real reading and the first big step toward literacy. The parents do not, at this point, conclude that their daughter likes to read, knows how to read, and therefore can now read on her own. Even though the girl is starting to read her own books, the parent/child relationship remains the key to the girl's progress. The young girl reads Dr. Seuss aloud to her parents, and concurrently Mom and Dad read Roald Dahl and J. K. Rowling to the girl (a nurturing combination of Q & A and PDP). By age 9 or 10, Mom and Dad fade from the scene, and the girl reads about Willie Wonka and Harry Potter all by herself (Independent Reflection).

Participant-Directed Processing allows people to experiment with various processing techniques while still under the supervision of a facilitator. It requires the same type of stepping-stone approach as learning to read. The whole reason for creating a concept called PDP was to give a name to the processing techniques that reside between Q & A and IR. PDP is a bridge to gradually take participants of experiential education programs from facilitator-controlled processing to processing on their own.

When the primary purpose of processing is to bring out the predetermined goals and objectives, training people to be more reflective remains in the background. PDP brings this secondary reason for processing to the forefront. When, for example, a facilitator has participants spend 15 minutes writing in their journals, he may be asking people to put their immediate thoughts and feelings to paper, but he is just as strongly promoting a lifelong habit of writing in journals.

Conclusion

Steve Simpson lived in Taiwan for 2 years, and during that time he met a Chinese-American painter who had moved to Taiwan to study Chinese brush strokes. Born and raised in the United States, the woman came to Asia primarily to study art, but she also wanted to get a sense of her Chinese heritage. Unfortunately, she stayed for only 2 months of what was supposed to be 12 months of study. The Chinese method of art education, at least at the school where she studied, was to study the Chinese masters. Her teachers told her that for her year in Taiwan, she would do nothing except study the brush strokes of famous painters and then try to replicate Chinese masterpieces. The woman, however, wanted to experiment. She wanted to take creative chances, maybe blend her Western training with Chinese brush techniques. She certainly did not want to spend her entire Asian experience copying other artists' works, so she packed her bags and went home to California.

When Steve discussed the woman's situation with a group of Chinese educators, one of them said, "This does not surprise me. It is representative of the differences in the two education systems. In traditional Confucian education, we do an excellent job of teaching students what to do, but we do not necessarily tell them why they should do it. In fact, the 'Why?' which comes so quickly from the lips of an American student is considered rude by many Chinese teachers. I am guessing that one reason the young artist went back to the United States is that she was seen as impertinent by her instructors here. Confucian education teaches students what to think, but not how to think. In the West, you do the exact opposite. You teach students how to think, but not what to think. In fact, students get criticized if they don't constantly question information, and teachers give credence to student opinions, even if they are not worth much. Some of this I find a bit odd. Still, if I had to choose, I think I prefer the Western system. It is important to teach students how to think."

Steve replied, "Thank you for the compliment about my educational system, but you give it too much credit. Western educators want to believe that they teach their students to think critically and be creative, but I'm not sure that we necessarily know how to do it. I would agree that we encourage students to think independently, but we don't always give them the skills to do it effectively. One of the reasons that some student opinions are not very good is that these students were not taught techniques for forming and expressing an opinion. They were just asked to do it. I am sure that an atmosphere that encourages questioning is helpful, but sometimes I think that there needs to be more direction."

Steve's story about the Chinese-American artist has relevance because the Chinese educator's comments about Chinese education and Western education are much like the comments experiential educators sometimes make about traditional education and experiential education. Traditional education does a good job of establishing a factual foundation; experiential education does a good job of putting that information to practical use. Of the two, experiential education also may do the better job of encouraging students to question what they have learned.[3] Does experiential education, however, merely ask students to question—or does it also show them how to question intelligently?[4] Contemplation, critical thinking, analysis, debriefing, processing—whatever it is called, education, and especially experiential education, have a responsibility of not only encouraging students to reflect and think critically, but also teaching them how to do it. It is as simple as that.

Reaching the Pinnacle

Processing is like driving with a manual transmission. When it is done well, the passengers barely notice the shifting of gears. When it is done poorly, the engine stalls and every-thing comes to a jarring stop.

When Steve Simpson lived in Taiwan, his apartment was in Taipei, a metropolitan area of over six million people. Not surprisingly, he and his wife, Hsieh Manyu, often left the city for short respites, and usually these outings were to Taiwan's Central Mountain Range. On one of these trips, they traveled to the resort town of Alishan. In Alishan, it is tradition to wake up before dawn and find a high point from which to watch the sun-rise. On their first morning there, Steve and Manyu climbed out of bed an hour before sunrise and hiked 30 minutes to the top of nearby Chushan (Celebration Mountain). The view from the summit was spectacular. The emerging predawn light revealed a long stretch of Taiwan's granite backbone and a mountain range of at least 30 different peaks.

In addition to the hiking trail to the top of Chushan, a narrow gauge railroad track ran within 150 meters of the summit. About 15 minutes before sunrise, a small tourist train pulled up to the end of the tracks, and nearly 200 Chinese tourists climbed out of the train and joined Steve and Manyu at the viewing area. Once all of the tourists had disembarked, a young tour guide climbed up onto a stone wall and, with the help of a battery-powered megaphone, delivered an interpretative talk. He identified the names of some of the bigger mountains in the vista, and he talk-ed about the wonder of the famous "Alishan sun appearance." He was a polished speaker, and he had his audience laughing at least a half dozen times during the short presentation.

Steve, however, did not enjoy the interpretative program. Although he was not so naïve as to think that a couple hundred people jammed on top of a mountain was going to be a personal and mystical encounter with nature, neither did he think that the event needed to be frontloaded by a comedic tour guide. In Steve's mind, awaiting the sunrise should have been at least a little introspective, and the guide would have served his audience better by having them quietly look at the view. While Steve did nothing to disrupt the interpretative monologue, he wanted to jump up on the rock wall and shout, "Hey Megaphone Man, what are you doing? Don't you know that the mountains speak for themselves?"

Soon after sunrise, everyone except Steve and Manyu headed back to the train, and the steam engine chugged off for the second tourist attraction of the morning.* Steve and Manyu were left alone at the mountaintop, but instead of relishing the solitude of the moment, Steve sat there wondering why he had been so quick to criticize the tour guide. Shouldn't the man have been complimented? He had, after all, infused education into what was clearly a case of mass tourism. At a gathering where there was little chance for anyone to experience the mystique of the mountains, the man had at least told the people what they should be watching for when the sun peaked over the distant ridge.

After a few minutes of reflection, Steve concluded that his frustration had been misdirected and that it wasn't even the tour guide that had bothered him. The young man just happened to be an easy target and was a messenger much more than a message. Steve was troubled because the sunrise, the tour guide, and the group of tourists had combined to create an event that left him doubting one of his basic beliefs about environmental

---

* Fifteen minutes after the sun appeared, people piled back into the train and headed for Monkey Rock, a 10-meter-high boulder shaped a little bit like a monkey. Steve's trip was in 1993; in 1999, an earthquake destroyed the railroad tracks to Monkey Rock, so currently it is not part of the Alishan tour package.

education and experiential education. He had just assumed that nature on her own was a better teacher than he ever could be, and whenever possible, he should step out of the way and let nature tell her own story. In other words, let the mountains and the trees and animals and *the sunrise* speak for themselves. Maybe Steve had taken the notion of Mountains Speak for Themselves (i.e., Independent Reflection) too literally, but if dawn atop a beautiful mountain overlooking a vista of distant mountain peaks is not a natural display that speaks for itself, is there *ever* any experience when a facilitator should keep his mouth shut and not try to improve upon the moment? Steve looked toward the sun, its orb now fully above the horizon, and asked, "If not now, when?"

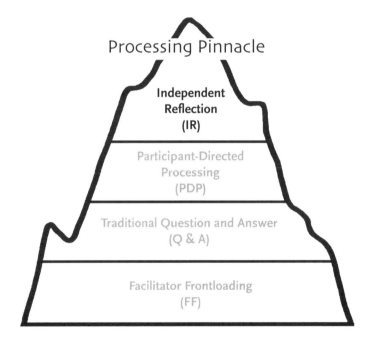

If Not Now, When?

Steve's story about Alishan is a long-winded way to ask whether there is ever a time and place where a facilitator should forego formal processing and let participants reflect entirely on their own. This is an excellent question. Obviously, people in their daily lives independently reflect on significant experiences, but how often do facilitators in an education setting intentionally skip a processing session because they believe the absence of formal processing provides the better learning experience? This is not to say that such independent reflection does not have an appealing, even romantic, feel to it. Who wouldn't like to take students to places of natural splendor and allow the power of nature to touch individuals on a personal level? Who wouldn't like to facilitate experiences so compelling that the lessons are self-evident and formal processing is unnecessary? On the other hand, are such experiences so rare in day-to-day experiential education that formal processing is always the more reliable way to go?*

In our opinion, Independent Reflection not only *should* be a part of a facilitator's processing repertoire, but it *must* be a part of it. Without IR, a facilitator's bag of techniques is incomplete. One end of the spectrum is missing. Even though it might get used rarely, IR is the appropriate processing methodology when a particular set of conditions has been met. If it is accepted that facilitators should control processing sessions only to the extent that facilitator guidance is necessary, then there will be times and situations where no formal processing is the appropriate facilitator action. The conditions for IR include

- AN APPROPRIATE SETTING. For IR to work well, the immediate surroundings should put participants in a reflective
  mood. The setting can be a simple place, such as a quiet

---

* Even Mountains Speak for Themselves (MST), the Outward Bound terminology that has come to mean the absence of formal processing, originated
simply as a criticism of outdoor trip leaders who tended to turn every
processing opportunity into a verbal counseling session.[1] Outward Bound
instructor Rusty Baillie recommended that leaders sometimes just let an
experience be appreciated for what it was—not a metaphor for something
else, not a lesson to be applied somewhere down the road, not a starting point for counseling—but a self-contained learning opportunity that
contributed to an interesting life. From Baillie's perspective, MST might include processing, just not overprocessing and/or convoluted interpretation.

spot next to a creek or a softly lit room with mellow music. It also can be a place so spectacular that it moves people to reverential silence. Great religious buildings (e.g., European cathedrals, Middle Eastern mosques, Asian temples) and stunning pristine nature fall into this second category. The best settings, whether subtle or spectacular, are not just quiet, but are out of the ordinary and distinctive from the urban and suburban banalities that can dull the reflective mind.[2]

Condition No. 1
for Independent Reflection
is an appropriate setting.

- PARTICIPANT COMMITMENT TO THE EXPERIENCE. A peaceful setting alone is not enough for the majority of people to slip into independent reflection. Steve's Alishan experience is a case in point. There also needs to be a commitment by the participants that marks the experience as significant. To some extent, the experience must be earned. This does not mean that the action component of the experience has to be physically or mentally difficult; rather it means that the participants have to take an active part in making the experience happen. An IR opportunity is more likely to occur by hiking to the top of a mountain than by taking a train there. It is more likely to occur when a moose is sighted on a week-long canoe trip than when a moose is seen at a zoo. Even though trains and zoos are viable forms of recreation, they do not promote reflection in the way that a more self-reliant experience might. Independence and self-sufficiency contribute to a reflective state. Participants who are dependent during the action component of an experience are apt to be dependent during the reflective component as well.

Condition No. 2
for Independent Reflection
is participant commitment to the experience.

- REQUISITE KNOWLEDGE. It is possible for someone to be in a special place and to have made a personal commitment to an experience, but still not appreciate the significance of everything that is happening. Much of experiential education, after all, is putting people in novel situations, and once outside of their everyday surroundings, people may not possess the background information that is needed to self-process the experience. Before facilitators choose to follow an action component of an experience with IR, they must decide if the participants' past experiences have prepared them for reflecting on the present moment. Facilitators must determine to what extent the experience has taken the participants outside of the norm. If only slightly beyond, then self-reflection or IR may make sense. If well beyond, the participants will need guidance from a wiser and more experienced authority. Clifford Knapp, in the book *Exploring the Power of Solo, Silence, and Solitude*, points out that even young Native Americans on a vision quest rely on medicine men and women to interpret their dreams and visions. Even though the commitment of the young person is very strong, the vision quest is so out of the ordinary that novices lack a foundation upon which to draw meaning. Only an elder of extraordinary knowledge can guide the young person to the deeper significance of the event.[3]

Condition No. 3
for Independent Reflection
is that when an important experience occurs
the participants have the requisite knowledge
to understand its significance.

- TRAINING IN PROCESSING. A purpose of the Processing Pinnacle model is to show that processing is a progression that may culminate in IR. In other words, experiential education facilitation takes participants through a series of processing methodologies. Each successive methodology works to the extent that the earlier methodologies have taught the participants something about processing. Each successive methodology assumes that participants gradually come to appreciate the value of processing and develop the tools to assume greater responsibility for the success of the processing session. The culmination or "pinnacle" of this processing training is the reality of participants who are able and willing to process entirely on their own.

Condition No. 4
for Independent Reflection
is that participants have the processing skills and
the motivation to process on their own.

A Daunting Set of Conditions

A reasonable response to this list of conditions is, "Criminy, that list is impossible. If all of that stuff has to be in place before I use IR, then, with the clientele I serve and with the limited time that I have with them, I will never actually use it." Our response, however, is, "That's right, and that is why IR is so seldom used in facilitated programing. But another way of looking at IR is to acknowledge that self-processing is going to happen regardless of how the facilitator handles his or her processing sessions. IR is inevitable. The only question is whether it occurs within a structured program or after the program is over. Isn't, after all, reflection in the absence of a facilitator really Independent Reflection?"

Most learning opportunities do not occur under the guidance of a facilitator. They happen during the unfacilitated experiences of life—experiences on the job, on the playground, while on vacation, etc. If these experiences are processed, and too often they are not, then they are self-processed. In other words, they are processed as a form of IR. When Steve, for example, sat atop Chushan and thought about the Alishan sun appearance, that was IR. No facilitator was asking him questions, but the questions came to him almost as if there were. Some fortunate people might be innately reflective; in Steve's case, he reflected because he had been formally trained in processing. One job of experiential education is to teach people to want to process.

Each time facilitators use IR in an educational setting, they are setting an example for the self-processing that occurs in everyday life. They are giving participants a chance to practice a skill that they will use after breaking ties with the facilitator. Most people, when outside the confines of a facilitated program, are not going to circle up their friends for a sharing circle, but they will find a coffee shop, church, or quiet spot in the woods to think about things that happened to them that day. Unless a facilitator's clientele includes people in a long-term care facility, the facilitator-participant relationship will eventually end. Hopefully participants leave that relationship in a more reflective state of mind.

A Processing Leap of Faith?

Even though IR is the least restrictive of all processing methodologies, facilitators tend not to use it. One reason is that facilitators want to hear what participants are thinking about. Even when facilitators have faith that participants will reflect on an experience, they still want assurance that the reflection is heading in a productive direction. Because IR seeks no feedback from participants, the facilitator often is left in the dark as to what is going on inside the participants' minds. The facilitator is surrounded by people who have formed opinions about an experience, but because there is no required public discourse, that facilitator has to trust that the unspoken reflection is sound and needs no elaboration. This is a bit unsettling to a facilitator accustomed to wringing lessons out of experience. It is more reassuring for the facilitator to round the group up and have a quick processing activity, not so much to analyze individual reflections as to confirm that quality reflection is taking place. The use of IR is more than trusting that participants will self-process; it is also feeling comfortable with not knowing the results of that self-processing. IR is an unspoken declaration of, "Okay, you're ready, and you're on your own now."

Stated this way, IR is a leap of faith—a leap that a reasonable facilitator might not see any reason to take. Is the risk worth the potential gain? Why not go right up to the edge of IR without making the final jump? Why not use processing techniques that give participants a great deal of freedom, but still require them to talk about their thoughts? Why can't IR be an idealistic target that is worked toward but intentionally never reached?

The answer to this question is that IR is the closest approximation to everyday life that a facilitated program can achieve. For facilitators reluctant to take the leap, it might be useful to appreciate the distinctions between IR and processing methodologies that come close to IR. These would be the techniques categorized as PDP. Obviously, the lines between the processing categories are fuzzy (the range of processing techniques is more of a continuum than a set of mutually exclusive boxes), but each category does have elements that distinguish it from the others. In determining whether a facilitator inches up to the IR precipice or takes the leap, consider the summary of differences between PDP and IR:

- PARTICIPANT-DIRECTED PROCESSING TENDS TO BE GROUP ORIENTED, WHILE INDEPENDENT REFLECTION IS LARGELY INDIVIDUAL. PDP is group processing without the constant guidance of a facilitator, and IR is individual processing without input from fellow group members. People captivated by a sunrise who individually drift off into their own reflective worlds is IR. A group of people sitting in a circle and discussing their reactions to a sunrise is PDP. Individuals wandering off on their own to write in their journals is IR. People sitting around a campfire to read from their journals is PDP.

- PARTICIPANT-DIRECTED PROCESSING TENDS TO BE AN ACTIVITY SET UP BY A FACILITATOR, WHILE INDEPENDENT REFLECTION IS INITIATED INDIVIDUALLY. As an example of PDP, a facilitator spreads out a set of pictures (e.g., processing cards, a large set of postcards), then asks every person to choose one and explain how it represents his or her role in the last activity. Conversely, IR is a person on a backpacking trip wandering off from the group campfire just to have time to herself. IR also is a person in a hotel room, just before bed, picking up the Gideon Bible, randomly picking a passage, and relating the reading to the events of the day. PDP involves a nudge from a facilitator; IR does not.

- PARTICIPANT-DIRECTED PROCESSING INCLUDES PUBLIC DISCLOSURE OF THE REFLECTIVE PROCESS, WHILE INDEPENDENT REFLECTION NEED NOT BE SHARED WITH OTHERS. A person who self-processes (i.e., uses IR to process) may voluntarily express his thoughts, but there is no intentional effort to draw out those thoughts.

- PARTICIPANT-DIRECTED PROCESSING TENDS TO BE A LESSON IN THE ART OF PROCESSING, WHEREAS INDEPENDENT REFLECTION IS APPLYING THE LESSON TO SELF-PROCESSING. PDP is a precursor to IR. If PDP, along with Traditional Q & A and possibly even Facilatator Frontloading, teaches people the importance of processing and the methods for self-processing, IR will follow.

Conclusion

There is no right answer as to when and where experiential educators should use IR. Undoubtedly, some freewheeling facilitators jump to IR before most members of a group have the skills to self-process. Just as likely, many cautious facilitators fail to use IR even when a particular group in a particular situation is ready for it.

But to be honest, it really does not matter much when and where individual facilitators decide to use IR. It really is a judgment call. What is important is that facilitators at least consider IR, even if they rarely use it in their programing. IR is important because it represents a faith in experiential learning. It is a belief that unique opportunities happen through experience and, given the right conditions, people draw memorable and unique lessons from these opportunities on their own.

The interesting part of Steve's Alishan sun appearance is not the event itself, but his reaction to it. This unusual, but hardly extraordinary, set of circumstances contradicted Steve's way of thinking, forcing him to question that way of thinking and alter it somewhat. Steve realized that had he walked to the top of Chushan as a facilitator with an organized group instead of his wife, he probably would have processed the event and his reaction to the tour group. He would have circled up his students and started asking questions about the tour group and its guide. He would have processed the shortcomings of mass tourism. In other words, he would have forced his reaction to the experience on the people he was supervising. This would have been his prerogative as a facilitator, but would it have been good facilitation? Steve's wife, Manyu, had not been bothered by the tour guide. She thought he was funny and, more importantly, she had not let the tour guide or the large group of people disrupt her appreciation of the mountains and the sunrise. And even though Manyu's reaction to events seems more typical than Steve's, Steve would have been so absorbed in his own thoughts that he probably would have made them a central focus of a Q & A session. And then what would have happened? Either the people of the group would have respected Steve's authority and followed him along the path that he was asking them to take, or one of them would have stepped in and asked why, atop a beautiful mountain on a beautiful morning, Steve was ignoring the reason that they had come. Didn't he know that the mountains speak for themselves?

Conclusion

Processing is like sowing an apple seed.
The planter may be around to see the seed germinate,
but could be long gone before the tree bears fruit.

Years have passed since Yangtze and McKinley last went on a backcountry trip together. Both have married, and Yangtze has two young children. McKinley stopped teaching rock climbing nearly 5 years ago, moved to Rochester, Minnesota, and is a trainer for a large corporation. Yangtze, even though she was more the wanderer of the two, has lived in the same town for nearly 10 years. She still works at the same university as she did before, but no longer runs the outdoor recreation center. Instead she assumed the newly created position of campus-wide internship and service learning coordinator. When the annual conference of the National Society for Experiential Education (NSEE) was being held in St. Paul, Yangtze called McKinley and he drove up to the Twin Cities one night to meet her for dinner.

Yangtze: My service learning position is only half time, so I get to spend a lot of time with my kids. My husband can set his own hours at work, so we don't even have to depend on day care. It's not the outdoorsy life I had when you and I were doing trips, but it's still very good.

McKinley: Good? It sounds perfect. You've hit the American dream trifecta. One, you have a great family. Two, you have a career that doesn't suck the life out of you. And three, you've found the good life without compromising any of your principles. How many people who went into experiential education because they loved the work can say they still are in experiential education 10 years later? I'm envious.

Yangtze: Thanks, I'm flattered. I think that I am doing worthwhile work. The school I work at is pretty traditional, so if not for internships and service learning, some of the kids wouldn't get any practical experience at all. But what about your job? Isn't what you are doing experiential education?

McKinley: Experiential education? In my own mind, I quit experiential ed when I stopped wearing a T-shirt to work. I equate experiential education so much with the outdoors that I never thought of HR as experiential education.

Yangtze: HR?

McKinley: Human Resources. I left the natural resources for human resources. I gave up the mountains for conference rooms. The pay is better, and I get to have dinner with my wife every night.

Yangtze: You didn't answer the question. Is what you do experiential education?

McKinley: I suppose it is. What I do is training, and it's hands on, but it's definitely different from before. Do you remember that last Association for Experiential Education conference we both went to, and you and I had that argument about the processing model that looked like a mountain?

Yangtze: The Processing Pinnacle. Sure, I remember it.

McKinley: Yeah, that's the model. Well, I still think the mountain imagery works well, and the best way to describe my job in terms of experiential education is to say that I mostly work from the base of the Processing Pinnacle. If I remember the model right, the base was all about the facilitator being in control, and the top of the pinnacle, where you did most of your stuff, was where the students had control. Well, my work now is 90% facilitator controlled. The goals are very specific, and I have folks only for a short time, usually only half a day. Other than frontloading the heck out of my training sessions, there isn't much processing. Even when I close up a workshop, it's not so much a reflection of the day as it is another chance for me to restate the purpose of the training. You'd find the whole thing pretty controlling.

Facilitators maintain control of the processing when it is vitally important that all participants appreciate the predetermined goals and objectives.

Yangtze: Not as much as I would have a few years ago. In my new job, I have two kinds of students—those on internship and those doing service learning projects. Students on internship are all over the country, so they have to keep journals of their experiences. Students on service learning projects stay in town, so they meet with me as a group once a week. At first, I figured that college students doing interesting things would be able to process on their own. But that's not true. They need help. Now, I actually conduct training sessions in journal writing before students go out on their internships. And even then, I have to critique their early journal entries to tell them what they are doing wrong. And my weekly meetings with the service learning students—well, I sequence my processing techniques just like the Processing Pinnacle suggests. At first I am as authoritative as you are in your job, but then I gradually teach them to process independently. I still think that the Processing Pinnacle, like most models, is too rigid, but I'll now admit that buried within the model is some good stuff.

> Facilitators should control processing sessions only to the extent that facilitator guidance is necessary.

McKinley: Once you have the rabbit, you can forget about the snare.

Yangtze: What?

McKinley: It's a Chinese proverb.* It means that words cannot adequately express ideas, but they're all we have to communicate with each other. Because words are only an approximation of an idea, we use them only until we understand the idea. Once we understand the idea, we don't need the words. Or in this case, once we understand the concept, we don't need the model. Processing is an intuitive practice, and the Processing Pinnacle is an attempt to put logic and structure to something that is not particularly logical. If, however, you reject the model offhand, you disregard the important concepts it

---

* The quote is from Chuang-tze. It goes, "The rabbit snare exists because of the rabbit; once you've gotten the rabbit, you can forget the snare. Words exist because of meaning; once you've gotten the meaning, you can forget the words." Chuang Tzu. 1968. *The Complete Works of Chuang Tzu*, trans. Burton Watson. New York: Columbia University Press, Chapter 26.

tries to represent. Better to capture the concepts first, then dump the model.

Yangtze: I guess I haven't dumped it, yet. It's still on my mind after all these years. It's like a bad dream, but it's there.

McKinley: So what are the important concepts? Figure those out, and we can both move past the model.

Yangtze: Well, the thing that stands out, because it was the thing that most bothered me years ago, is that it downplays spontaneity. It ran contrary to the way that I processed at the time, which was having a grab bag of processing activities handy, then using them when and how the moment moved me. Instead of spontaneity, the Pinnacle called for a planned sequence of processing methods. It started out with the experiential educator controlling everything, then gradually delegating responsibility to the students.

The Processing Pinnacle is a planned sequence of processing techniques.

McKinley: I mostly agree with your point, although I think that you are interpreting the Pinnacle too literally. It was never an inflexible step-by-step procedure. Leaders still need to read the moods, abilities, and attention spans of their followers, and then choose the appropriate processing technique. The top of the mountain is the goal, but the path to the top is not straight up the mountainside. Routes dip and turn; they poke above the tree line, then dip back down below it. Leaders misread signs, arrive at dead ends, and have to backtrack. People regress when they face new challenges; they

Processing plans cannot be carved in stone, because quality processing requires facilitators to read and adjust to the unique characteristics of the situation.

sometimes just get tired. The Processing Pinnacle identifies the stages and the desired final destination, but it does not lay out the exact path.

Yangtze: That description fits my job right now. I want my students to process on their own, but they are all over place. Some processed well before I ever met them, some never get it, and others go up and down, back and forth. And I adjust my leadership accordingly, just like you say.

McKinley: Okay, processing techniques can be set up in a planned sequence. What else?

Yangtze: Another obvious one for me is that a goal of processing is to teach people how to process, not just what to process. My students do a dozen different things and learn dozens of different lessons. I can't tell each of them what to learn, but I can teach them how to process so that they can figure it out for themselves.

When educators promote a life of experiencing, they must teach their students how to reflect on those experiences.

McKinley: But that doesn't describe what I'm doing right now. It would be great if my trainees learned to process on their own, but that's not why I process. It's all about learning the specific goals and objectives of the training session. All of the people in a particular class are supposed to learn exactly the same thing, and unless all of them can take very specific skills back to their departments, I've failed in my responsibility.

Yangtze: So the goals of processing change according to the needs of the students— and as the goals of processing change, so do the processing methods. Sometimes processing is to help people process specific experiences, and sometimes it is to teach people processing skills so they can reflect independently on future experiences.

McKinley: And sometimes it's something else altogether. The important part is that the processing method should be one that works well for accomplishing that specific purpose.

Yangtze: Right, but regardless of the reasons behind the processing, educators need to get out of the way once people can process on their own. Use Independent Reflection once people are ready to reflect independently.

McKinley: There's some irony for you. You, the person who hated the Processing Pinnacle, are adhering to its principles more than I am.

Yangtze: If that's true, it's because my thinking now coincides with some things in the model, not because the model did anything to change me. Maybe I am mellowing in my old age. I admit that I used to turn people loose before they had the skills to process. When I was running rivers with people, I couldn't see it. Spending time in nature was an end in itself, so once I had people outdoors, processing was an add-on, and I didn't care too much what kind of reflection came out of it. Now that my goals are more complicated and more varied, the processing takes on greater significance.

When I want my students to link their practical experiences to the classroom and to their obligations as citizens, I am finding out that many of them can't do it on their own. I have to teach processing and gradually lead them to self-reflection.

McKinley: You're mellowing, and I'm getting even less so. You're making me think that I'm too strict in my teaching. The people that I teach are more experienced and probably more mature than your college students, yet I don't give them the freedom that you do.

Yangtze: No, it's all situational. You're doing on-the-job training, and I'm contributing to a liberal arts education. We're after two different outcomes. I am helping students to understand why their experiences are worthwhile. For the employees you work with, that should be self-evident.

McKinley: That's interesting. I just assumed that processing moved up the Pinnacle according to the skill level of the participants, but that's not necessarily so. My trainees are very skilled, but I'm working from the base of the Pinnacle, and I might stay at the base of the Pinnacle indefinitely. Since I have specific desired outcomes and I have people only for a very short period of time, I keep control of the processing.

Yangtze: And my students are green, but I can process with them higher up on the Pinnacle. I was critical of the model because it was hierarchical. I thought it meant that people who achieved Independent Reflection were smarter or better than everyone else, but that's not true. The difference is the purpose of the experience and, to some extent, the time factor. Because my outcomes are more varied than yours, I have the luxury of greater freedom in my processing. Also, because I have an entire semester, not just a couple of hours, I can set aside time to actually teach people how to process more effectively. I have time to help them up the Processing Pinnacle. I probably spend more time teaching people how to process than you spend in your entire program.

Teaching people to process takes time.

McKinley: Although the open-endedness of your processing is partly a reflection of your personality, you also are doing it out of necessity. You have a bunch of people all working toward different goals, yet it's not practical for you to process with each of them individually. For practicality's sake, you have to teach people to process on their own. It's your only option.

Yangtze: Either I teach them to process on their own or some of the valuable lessons of their experiences get lost. Their experiences occur when I'm not even present.

McKinley: And because you taught them to self-process, you can assume that processing is happening when you aren't around. I don't do that with my trainees.

Truly teaching people to process means that they will process even if no facilitator is present.

Yangtze: Because, in your job, that is not a priority.

McKinley: But should it be? Am I shortchanging my trainees by controlling everything?

Yangtze: Only if the needs of your trainees change. So long as the need is to learn the specific skill that you are teaching, the processing is right. If your goals expand, then so too should your processing.

McKinley: Pretty good insights. Have we internalized enough from the Processing Pinnacle model that we can now get rid of it?

Yangtze: For me, it's already forgotten.

McKinley: You always were a little quicker to move ahead than I was. Give me a few days to sit on it.

Yangtze: Not quicker than you; just more impulsive. Take your time.

Appendix A   A Few Processing Activities

In this first of two appendices to *The Processing Pinnacle*, we offer a handful of processing techniques that have worked well for us. A couple of the techniques (the Great Fortune Cookie Trick and the Anonymous Continuum) are of our own invention. The rest (Dyads, Concept Maps, and Processing Cards) describe our approach to well-established practices.

The five techniques are identified as being Facilitator Frontloading, Traditional Question and Answer, or Participant-Directed Processing. This is done to encourage facilitators to think of their favorite processing techniques in terms of a progression. There are no techniques listed as Independent Reflection. Independent Reflection is usually initiated by the individual participants, not the facilitator. In our minds, Independent Reflection, from the facilitator's perspective, is an opportunity (a special moment, time, and place) more than a specific technique.

Obviously, this is a limited list of activities. If the reader is looking specifically for a collection of techniques, there are books with more extensive lists than the short one offered here. For example, *Reflective Learning*[1] and *A Teachable Moment*[2] are primarily technique books. Combined, these two books give an experiential educator over 150 processing techniques to choose from. A hundred fifty processing techniques! That should give someone, who up until now has limited his or her processing to straightforward question and answer, something to work from.

Facilitator Frontloading Technique

The Great Fortune Cookie Trick

The Great Fortune Cookie Trick, like most of our wackiest ideas, came to us while driving home in the dead of night after a TEAM conference.* It is not so much a processing technique as it is a way to dress a metaphor. We should point out that the Great Fortune Cookie Trick requires facilitator deception, although we prefer to call it magic.

Equipment Needed
- One deck of Chiji Processing Cards** (or other metaphoric card deck)
- A stash of fortune cookies (at least one cookie/participant)
- Lots and lots of fortunes based on the processing cards (see instructions below)

Directions
1. At the very beginning of a workshop (works best if it is at least a half-day program), spread out the full deck of Chiji Processing Cards. Tell the group that they must pick a card that will represent the group for the day. It does not matter how the card is chosen, but there must be consensus (i.e., every single person in the group must agree to the card before the group can move on). After the group has chosen a card, it must explain to the facilitators the symbolism of the card. (For example, the group chooses the wheel, because each person is one spoke of a greater whole. Every person brings unique skills, and together all of the participants can be something that they could not be individually.)

---

* TEAM is Teachers of Experiential and Adventure Methodology, an annual conference hosted by Northeastern Illinois University, a commuter school on the far north side of Chicago. For us, it is a treat at the tail end of winter, an eclectic blend of experiential education, physical education, spirituality, and Native American culture. Interested experiential educators can check the conference out at http://www.neiu.edu/~team/index.htm.

**See page 151 for an explanation of Chiji Processing Cards.

Note: If the group is larger than 10 people, Step 1 can be done in rounds. For example, with a group of 20 people, create three groups. Each group of approximately seven is given a deck of cards and asked to pick its representative card. Then the groups come together, and spokespersons from the groups must explain why their card represents the group. Finally all the groups must agree on a single card, either one of the three cards chosen in the small groups or another card altogether.

2. From that point on, the workshop facilitators frequently refer to the metaphor card chosen by the group (e.g., instead of asking people to form a circle, they are asked to form a wheel; instead of asking people to identify their contribution to a specific initiative, the facilitator draws a wagon wheel on the chalkboard and asks people to name the spoke they were during the previous initiative). In other words, facilitators repeatedly dress the metaphor.

3. Sometime during the workshop, one of the facilitators slips out of the room, out of sight of the participants. There he or she has stashed away a) fortune cookies from which the original fortunes have been carefully extracted with tweezers and b) multiple sets of customized fortunes. These fortunes correspond to the Chiji Cards. For example, one set of fortunes represents the eagle card and consists of 20+ individual fortunes, each reading "Be the eagle." Another set of 20+ fortunes represents the sunset card and each fortune reads "Be the sunset." And, of course, there are 20+ fortunes that correspond with the card that the group chose at the beginning of the workshop (in our example, 20+ fortunes that read, "Be the wheel"). The facilitator puts all but the "Be the wheel" fortunes away for another day. Then he slides one "Be the wheel" fortune into each fortune cookie. There are now 20 fortune cookies with a fortune that reads "Be the wheel." The facilitator goes back to the group and nonchalantly puts a brown paper bag of fortune cookies over to one side.

4. At the conclusion of the workshop, part of the closure includes a facilitator saying, "Before we finish and go our separate ways, I have a small gift for each you. Nothing

special, just a fortune cookie. The fortune, however, is special. In fact, I believe that the fortune will speak to each of you in a personal way. The only thing that I ask is that you do not open your fortune cookie right now. Please wait at least 30 minutes and open it only when you have a couple minutes away from other people. Then open the cookie and reflect upon the fortune. That's all I ask." The cookies are dispensed as a small going-away gift, and 30 minutes later, individuals will independently open their fortunate cookies and read, "Be the wheel."

A Magician's Touch

Buzz once mentioned our fortune cookie trick to magician Jeff Lefton, and he immediately told us that the trick was a good one, but that it lacked showmanship. He said that our students are immediately going to figure out how the trick was done; they will correctly guess that one of us snuck out of the room and stuffed fortune cookies with the correct fortune. He suggested that we do a better job of setting up the illusion. Specifically we should have a bowl of fortune cookies setting out in plain sight during the entire workshop. We should have the cookies out and visible when the participants first enter the room. When the facilitator leaves the room to stuff the fortune cookies, he puts the cookies in a bowl that looks exactly like the bowl that is setting out in plain sight. Later, when the participants are momentarily out of the room (e.g., a toilet break), he switches the two bowls of fortune cookies—and now the fortune cookies in plain sight all have fortunes that read, "Be the wheel." When the participants receive their fortune cookies and read "Be the wheel," they will be stunned. "How did they do that? Those cookies were setting out even before we picked the wheel card."

Traditional Question and Answer Technique

The Anonymous Continuum*

The human continuum is a fairly common processing technique.** In it, the facilitator creates a long line (15-30 feet) on the ground. This line represents a continuum, one end "strongly agree," the other end "strongly disagree," and the middle ground various degrees of agreement and disagreement. As the facilitator asks opinion questions (e.g., How well did the group cooperate on the last initiative?), participants publicly place themselves on the continuum in response to the question. An example of the human continuum is described in chapter 2 of this book.

The Anonymous Continuum is a high-tech version of the human continuum. It utilizes PowerPoint and laser pens. Whereas the traditional human continuum requires that participants publicly declare their opinion, the anonymous continuum presents the group's overall sentiment without individuals in the group having to reveal their personal opinions to the rest of the group.

Equipment Needed
- Prepared PowerPoint presentation
- Projection equipment (computer and projector) for a PowerPoint presentation or a large flip chart if the technology is not available
- Laser pens (one pen/participant)

Directions
1. Prior to meeting with a group, the facilitator develops a series of continuum-like questions in a PowerPoint presentation. Most of the continua will simply have the two extreme

---

* The Anonymous Continuum was first used at "Three Steps to Better Processing," a workshop by Steve Simpson and Dan Miller at the annual Association for Experiential Education conference in Vancouver, British Columbia, November 2003.

** *Reflective Learning* describes this method of processing under the name "Continuum Exercises." Sugerman, D., Doherty, K., Garvey, D., and Gass, M. 2000. *Reflective Learning: Theory and Practice*. Dubuque, IA: Kendall/ Hunt, pp. 64-65.

answers to the question listed on either end (see Continuum No. 1). Some continua, however, will have a range of responses listed in the PowerPoint slide (see Continuum No. 2). Eight to 12 slides is a good number.

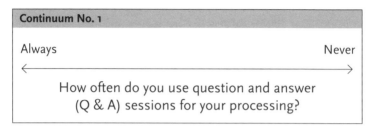

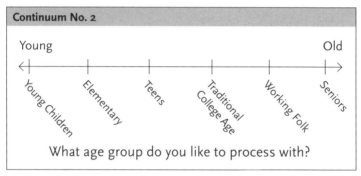

2. When it is time to process, each participant is given a laser light pen. Usually, the facilitator will have to give participants thirty seconds to shine their pens at everything except each other's eyes before proceeding.

3. The facilitator then shows the PowerPoint presentation. With each slide, he or she asks a question, and all of the participants answer the question by shining their laser pens at the appropriate spot on the screen. This differs from the human continuum in that it is difficult to determine where any individual is shining his or her laser beam. All that can be seen is the overall distribution of red dots.

4. Based upon the results of the survey, the facilitator summarizes the results and asks follow-up questions. Sometimes questions follow each slide; at other times questions come after all of the slides have been shown.

Participant-Directed Processing Technique

~~~~~~

Dyads*

We had a difficult time deciding whether dyads were Traditional Question and Answer or Participant-Directed Processing. We opted for PDP, because in our experience, participants in dyads use the facilitator questions only as a starting point. They usually digress so far from the initial question that it really is participant-directed. When the dyads regroup to summarize their discussions, participants usually start their comments by saying, "We didn't really answer the question that we were asked. Instead we talked about...."

The rationale for dyads is that people will feel more comfortable in smaller groups. They may be more open in a group of 2 to 5 people than in a group of 20 or more.

Equipment Needed
- At most, a written list of questions for each dyad

Directions
1. Instead of conducting a large group question and answer session, break the group up into smaller subgroups. Dyad means two, but the groups can be 2 to 5 people.

2. Then have these smaller groups discuss among themselves. Sometimes the facilitator simply gives them an open-ended subject to discuss. More often it is a list of 2 to 3 questions. If the questions were prepared beforehand, they can be submitted to the dyads on paper. If the questions were created spontaneously during the action component of the experience, they can be submitted orally.

---

* Dyads have been part of experiential education for a long time. We include it here because we mentioned them several times in the book. Tom Smith writes about dyads/triads in "Alternative Methodologies for Processing the Adventure Experience," a chapter in Gass, M., ed. 1993. *Adventure Therapy: Therapeutic Applications of Adventure Programming.* Dubuque, IA: Kendall/Hunt. They also are discussed in the short "Methods of Processing" section of Luckner, J. L., & Nadler, R. S. 1997. *Processing the Experience: Strategies to Enhance and Generalize Learning,* 2nd ed. Dubuque, IA: Kendall/Hunt, p. 119.

3. While not necessary, it is common to conclude the dyad activity by bringing everyone back together into a single group. Spokespersons from each dyad then summarize aloud the key points of the small group discussions.

   Tip: During small group discussion, some facilitators give the dyads privacy. Other facilitators practice LBWA (leadership by wandering around). In other words, they wander from group to group, catching small snippets of conversation. This encourages groups to stay on task.

Adaptation 1: Jen's Concentric Circles

For large groups, Jen Stanchfield of High5 Adventure Learning Center uses a well-known ice breaking activity to create multiple processing dyads. She begins with an inner circle and outer circle of people. The inner circle faces out and the outer circle in, so every person from the outer circle stands opposite a partner from the inner circle. These two people discuss a question, then the facilitator tells one of the circles to shift a couple people to the left, creating new pairs. The facilitator then gives everyone a new question to discuss.[*]

Adaptation 2: Dan's Balloons

Dan Miller adds a little fun to dyads by incorporating Fire in the Hole to the processing activity. When pairing up people for one-on-one discussions, he gives each pair an inflated balloon. They suspend the balloon between their bellies, then hug each other until the balloon pops. The twist is that Dan has inserted processing questions inside the balloon, so the pair has to pop the balloon to find out what to discuss.

---

[*] Concentric circles are described in detail in Cain, J., Cummings, M., and Stanchfield, J. 2005. *A Teachable Moment: A Facilitator's Guide to Activities for Processing, Debriefing, Reviewing and Reflection.* Dubuque, IA: Kendall/ Hunt, pp. 76-77.

Metaphoric Concept Maps

Concept maps are a visual form of dyads. While not unique to experiential education, they are an excellent tool for seeing how groups interpret the action component of an experience.* For those who teach in a traditional classroom, concept maps are a popular way to allow students to summarize the important points of a lecture or classroom activity.

Equipment Needed
*   Equipment to show drawings to large group. With technology rooms that have an opaque visualizer, paper and marking pens work well. Otherwise, large newsprint and marking pens or overhead projector, transparencies, and transparency pens.

Directions
1. Following the action component of an experience (e.g., group initiative, naturalist-led hike, lecture), have students get into groups of 3 to 5 people to discuss and summarize the most important concepts of the event. Also give the participants drawing supplies for sketching something that symbolizes the most important aspects of their discussion.

2. As you distribute the drawing materials, tell the groups that, after 10 to 15 minutes of small group discussion, each small group will tell the other groups about their discussion by displaying and explaining its concept map.

3. It may be helpful to students for the instructor to briefly define concept maps before sending them on their processing task. Concept maps are visual representations of concepts and ideas. Originally they were used in planning as a way

---

* Online sites describing concept maps include http://users.edte.utwente. nl/lanzing/cm_home.htm, http://www.graphic.org/concept.html, and http://classes.aces.uiuc.edu/ACES100/Mind/CMap.html

to get brainstorming to paper, but they work just as well at the completion of an action as a way to summarize the reflective process. Concept maps take several forms, and no form is any better than another. The two most common are flowchart or spider concepts maps (see Figure A.1) and picture or metaphoric concept maps (see Figure A.2).

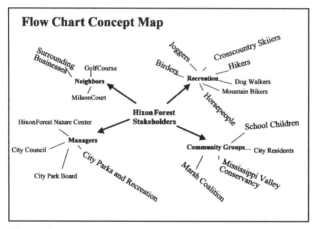

Figure A.1

Figure A.2

(Primarily) Participant-Directed Processing Technique

Processing Cards

The most useful item in a facilitator's processing kit probably is a generic list of good processing questions. The second most useful item might be a deck of processing cards. At their most basic, processing cards are excellent props for novice facilitators not yet comfortable with processing. Used in more elaborate ways, they also appeal to experienced educators. Processing cards are a collection of metaphoric images that can be spread out in front of a group. Some facilitators create their set of cards by compiling postcards or other  interesting pictures.* Others have one or more sets of the various commercially prepared decks. Chiji Processing Cards and Chiji Pocket Processor are two decks of processing cards that the three of us have created.** Michelle Cummings of Training Wheels and other professional facilitators also have designed comparable products and make them available through experiential education vendors.

Equipment Needed
• A deck of processing cards

---

* *Reflective Learning* describes the use of postcards. See Sugerman, D., Doherty, K., Garvey, D., & Gass, M. 2000. *Reflective Learning: Theory and Practice.* Dubuque: Kendall/Hunt, p. 87.

** All of our processing products carry the brand name "Chiji." Chiji is a Chinese word meaning "significant moment" or "turning point." It is an event that changes a person's life, and the direction of the change depends upon the individual's readiness and willingness to learn from the experience and act in response to it. Chi literally means "key," suggesting that if a person has the key, then the significant moment can be used to open doors to new and valuable opportunities. See www.chiji.com.

Directions

1. The most direct way to use processing cards is immediately after an experiential education activity. Spread the cards out face up so everyone can see all of the images. Then ask a question that each person is expected to answer. For example, the facilitator says, "Pick one card that describes your contribution to the last activity. Choose carefully because, in about 30 seconds, I am going to ask each of you to name your card and explain why you chose the card that you did."

2. After all participants have picked a card, each person takes his or her turn in naming and explaining his or her chosen card to the rest of the group. Usually the facilitator simply lets each person explain the metaphor derived from the card, but, if appropriate, the facilitator can ask a pertinent follow-up question to one or more of the participants.

Adaptation 1. Dyads

After the participants have picked their cards, the facilitator asks them to break into pairs to discuss their cards. One person explains his or her card, and the listener offers feedback on the explanation. Then roles are reversed. After these short discussions, participants return to the large group to explain their cards to everyone. The pairings allow participants to verbalize and get feedback on their ideas before publicly declaring them in a larger and perhaps more intimidating setting.

Adaptation 2. Identity Card

If creating a group identity is desired, the facilitator may want the participants to find a single card that best represents the group. Instead of asking each participant to find a card that describes him or her as an individual, the facilitator asks each person to pick a card that best represents the group as a whole. Let each person explain his or her choice. Then place all of the cards together (both the chosen cards and those not chosen) in the center of the group and instruct the participants to come to consensus as to the single card that best represented the group during the last activity. The choice should not be a vote, but a true consensus. Every participant has veto power, and no card represents the group until all participants accept the choice. Choosing the card then becomes an initiative in itself, so the facilitator should allow sufficient time for consensus decision making to occur.

Adaptation 3. A Focusing Tool

Processing cards are most often used to create a metaphor after the shared experience. They can be used, however, to create the metaphor up-front. During the intoduction of a program or activity, spread the cards out and ask participants to pick the card that best represents what they want to get out of the upcoming experience. Each individual can have his or her own metaphor, or the group can use consensus decision making to pick a single metaphor for the group.

Adaptation 4. Can I Ask the Question Now?

This idea actually came from a 12-year-old student whose teacher used processing cards in his classroom. After the students in class had used the cards to explain what they liked best about a particular activity, one of the students asked, "Do we get to ask a question now?" The teacher let a few members of the class ask questions, and it worked. If one purpose of processing is to shift the locus of control from the facilitator to the participants, letting the participants actually ask the questions is a good idea.

Adaptation 5. Then, Now, and Later

When people see processing cards for the first time, they often ask, "Are these like tarot cards or something?" Actually they are nothing like tarot cards, but they can be used by facilitators to elicit feelings about the past, present, and future. During a one-on-one session, a facilitator spreads out all of the processing cards. He or she then asks the participant to choose the card that best describes the way that she feels about herself today. After the participant explains the first card, the facilitator asks the participant to pick a second card, this one representing the way she felt about herself when she started the program. After that card has been explained, the facilitator asks the individual to pick a final card, this card representing how the participant wants to be at the completion of the program. Once completed, the three cards represent a picture of both the progress made and the distance yet to go.

Adaptation 6. Leisure Assessment

This idea comes from the Leisure Lifestyle Center at the University of Wisconsin-La Crosse. As part of the center's leisure education service, the staff often uses processing cards to conduct basic leisure assessments. It is an easy way to discover what clients understand about their leisure and their "free time." During a first meeting, the facilitator spreads out a deck of processing cards. A participant is then asked to pick a card that best represents such topics as 1) his favorite recreation activity, 2) the way he usually spends his free time, 3) reasons he likes to do his favorite activities, 4) the other people he recreates with, 5) the reasons (barriers to leisure) he does not participate in his favorite activity as often as he would like, 6) the activities that he has never done but would like to try, or 7) what he would like his leisure lifestyle to look like in the future. Whatever the question, the participant picks a card (or cards) and explains the rationale behind the choice. This exercise, while usually done during a one-on-one interview, can also be used in group sessions as well. And while this example is specifically a leisure assessment, facilitators can obviously use the same technique to encourage participants to talk about a wide range of subjects.

A good practice of experiential educators is to stockpile a list of favorite processing questions. While the questions in the list may be written in non-specific terms, it is from this list of generic questions that specific questions for a specific processing session can be developed. Rather than inventing new questions for each and every group, it makes more sense to generate a master list of good questions, then use that list to customize a short list for the specific situation.

The following is a list of questions that we have developed over the years. Some are questions that we thought up on our own. Others are tweaked versions of other published lists. Clifford Knapp's *Lasting Lessons*, for example, has pages of questions organized according to theme.[1] Luckner and Nadler's *Processing the Experience,* while it does not devote a special section for questions, does sprinkle short lists of interesting questions throughout its pages.[2] Our list of questions is broken down in two different ways. First of all, it is divided into 21 different themes. The themes certainly are not all-encompassing, but include subjects that we, and probably many experiential educators, encounter regularly. Second, each themed list is divided into the question types of fact finding, analysis/feelings, and synthesis/transference. This categorization is our attempt to adhere to Quinsland and Van Ginkel's suggestion that Q & A begins with easy, straightforward questions and works up to the questions that are most difficult to answer.[3]

Even though these questions are broken down into themes, they are intentionally non-specific. The questions are not associated with specific activities, nor are they aligned with a particular kind of clientele. Therefore they are not intended, in the majority of cases, to be used word for word. Even if readers like some of these questions, they still should reword them to fit the unique situation.

A Facilitator's Field Guide
Table of Contents

1 Doing Something I Didn't Think I Could

> "If you would have asked me this morning,
> I would have said that I wasn't going to do it."

Fact-Finding Questions

1. Who just did something that they thought they could not do?
2. What was it that you did?
3. Did anyone feel that they haven't been "tested" yet? Do you want to be? If so, what kind of challenge is missing?
4. Did anyone notice a special achievement by someone else? If so, what was it?

Analysis and Feeling Questions

5. What helped you to accomplish the difficult task?
6. What was the barrier that originally made you think that you couldn't do it?
7. Describe your feelings now that it is over.
8. Would you do it again? Why or why not?

Synthesis and Transference Questions

9. What does the term "a philosophy of experiencing" mean to you?
10. Give an example from everyday life when you did something that you didn't think you could do.
11. Give an example from everyday life when you backed away from trying something because you didn't think that you could do it.
12. Do you see differences between when you choose to take the risk and when you don't? If so, what are those differences?

Based upon the responses to some of these questions, the facilitator may want to conduct more in-depth discussions about whether:

- Some people are chance-takers and some are not.

- Risk taking is better than being cautious.
- A cautious person taking a small risk is actually more courageous than a risk-taker taking a big risk.
- The risks of today (fear of heights, fear of looking incompetent, etc.) are analogous to the fears of everyday life.
- People have perceived limits that are more mental than anything else.
- There is a time for taking risks and a time for being cautious.

Notes and Customized Questions

2 Feeling Proud

"I know that the purpose of these activities was to build self-esteem, and I have to admit that I feel pretty proud of myself."

Fact-Finding Questions

1. Let's go quickly around the circle. Each person describe one thing that you did today that makes you feel proud.

Analysis and Feeling Questions

2. What is it about these accomplishments that made you feel proud?
3. Do these various reasons for pride have anything in common? In other words, do the same things make each of you proud, or do each of you find pride in different kinds of things?
4. Pride is a double-edged sword. If it improves self-esteem, pride is considered a good thing. If self-esteem expands to the point that a person is arrogant and egotistical, then pride is considered bad. Was the pride you felt today good pride or bad pride? Explain.
5. Was the pride that you felt today at the expense of someone else? Explain.
6. What things did the group do to help each of us enhance our self-esteem?
7. What things did the group do to whittle away at people's self-esteem?

Synthesis and Transference Questions

8. Other than today, what else have you done that made you feel proud?
9. Has today's source of pride changed you in a way that will have an impact beyond today? Explain.
10. Contemporary society seems to value both pride and humility. If you value both pride and humility, explain how this is not a contradiction.

Based upon the responses to some of these questions, the facilitator may want to conduct more in-depth discussions about:

- Balance between pride and arrogance.
- Sources of low self-esteem.
- Differences between confidence and pride, between self-esteem and pride.

Notes and Customized Questions

3 Challenging Myself

> "I tend to stay within my personal comfort zone,
> but today was different because...."

Fact-Finding Questions

1. What does the term "comfort zone" mean to you?
2. Who moved beyond their comfort zone in this activity? Doing what?
3. Who today decided to stay within their comfort zone? What was one reason for doing so?

Analysis and Feeling Questions

4. How do you feel about yourself after stepping out of your comfort zone?
5. How do you feel about yourself after consciously choosing not to step out of your comfort zone?
6. For those who did step out their comfort zone, what allowed you to do it?
7. For those who did not step out of your comfort zone, what, if anything, prevented you from taking the chance?

Synthesis and Transference Questions

8. In experiential education, much is made about pushing yourself beyond your normal level of comfort. Is pushing yourself beyond what is comfortable important to you? Why or why not?
9. What is the value of stepping out of a comfort zone?
10. Should the people who did not move beyond their comfort level be pushed a little harder to do so? Why or why not?
11. If participants should be pushed a little harder, what suggestions do you have as to how to do this?
12. What are some good reasons for remaining in a place where you feel entirely comfortable?
13. Are you more apt to step out of your comfort zone here than in your day-to-day life? Why or why not?
14. What is one specific thing that you can do to step out of your comfort zone in everyday life?

Based upon the responses to some of these questions, the facilitator may want to conduct more in-depth discussions about whether:

- People should feel bad about themselves for not pushing themselves.
- A small step for some people (e.g., just getting on the ladder, just holding hands) is a greater challenge than something more spectacular done by others.

Notes and Customized Questions

4 Asking for Help

"I felt that I needed some help from the group.
I asked for it, and they came through."

Fact-Finding Questions

1. Give me three examples where someone from the group specifically asked for help.
2. How did members of the group respond to the requests?
3. Did anyone need help, but not ask for it? If so, what was the situation?
4. Is it okay to ask for help? Why or why not?

Analysis and Feeling Questions

5. Were the people who asked for help satisfied with the response from the group? Why or why not?
6. Of the people who needed help, but did not ask—why didn't you ask?
7. Can you offer any suggestions about when to assume people need help and when to wait for them to ask for help?

Synthesis and Transference Questions

8. Was it easier to ask for help during this activity than in everyday life? If so, what was the difference?
9. How do people in everyday life respond when you ask for help?
10. How do you respond when people in everyday life ask you for help?
11. Can you think of experiences in the past when your requests for help were rebuffed? What was the situation?

Based upon the responses to some of these questions, the facilitator may want to conduct more in-depth discussions about whether:

- People think that asking for help is a sign of weakness.
- Lack of trust or dislike for each other prevents asking for help.

- Past experiences have led to a "why bother?" attitude.
- People are more willing to help in a structured situation than in everyday life.
- There is a difference between asking for physical help and asking for emotional help.

Notes and Customized Questions

5 Sharing Information

> "He knew some stuff, and I knew some stuff,
> so together we were able to do it."

Fact-Finding Questions

1. What one piece of information did somebody have that everyone else needed in order to succeed in the last activity?
2. What would have taken longer—one person doing the activity alone or all of you doing the activity together? Explain.
3. What would have produced the better final product—one person doing the activity alone or all of you doing the activity together? Explain.

Analysis and Feeling Questions

4. What words best describe the willingness of people in the group to share important information?
5. What are reasons people hog information and keep it to themselves? What are the justifications for these reasons?

Synthesis and Transference Questions

6. Does anyone here remember sharing information or giving help to someone in everyday life and not receiving anything in return? What was the situation? How do you feel about it now?
7. Has anyone here shared information or given help to others, and in the long run, received much more than you gave? What was the situation? How do you feel about it now?
8. What are three things at _____ (e.g., home, school, work, the institution) that make you not want to share information with other people?

Based upon the responses to some of these questions, the facilitator may want to conduct more in-depth discussions about whether:

- People expect reciprocation when they share information.
- There are times when sharing information backfires.

- There is a link between trust and the willingness to share information.

Notes and Customized Questions

6 Talking to Each Other

"We actually talked to each other, and it helped us succeed."

Fact-Finding Questions

1. Who spoke most often during this activity?
2. Who were these talkers talking to? To the whole group? To certain individuals?
3. Were there any people who barely talked? If so, who were they?
4. How would you describe most of the talking? For example, was it discussion, asking questions, giving instructions, off the topic...?

Analysis and Feeling Questions

5. How did talking contribute to completing the task?
6. How did some of the talking distract from the completion of the task?
7. How did talking contribute to the dynamics of the group?
8. How did some of the talking hurt the dynamics of the group?

Synthesis and Transference Questions

9. Were the people who talked during this activity the same people who do most of the talking in other situations?
10. Talkers, why do you speak more than others?
11. Quieter people, why do you speak less than others?
12. Is it okay with you that the same people do most of the talking? How does it help or hinder the group?
13. Should we do anything different about who talks during the next activity? If so, what?

Based upon the responses to some of these questions, the facilitator may want to conduct more in-depth discussions about whether:

- The "talkers" are resented by others in the group for being pushy.

- The "quiet people" feel intimidated about discussing the subject of being quiet.
- An emotionally safe environment encourages discussion by all.

Notes and Customized Questions

7 Been There, Done That!

> "I was kinda bored, because
> I've done most of this stuff before."

Fact-Finding Questions

1. By a raise of hands, how many of you had done this activity before today?
2. For those of you who had done this activity before, what was your initial reaction when the leader started explaining the activity? How did it affect the way you participated?
3. For those of you who had not done this activity before, how did the people who had done it before affect the way you felt about it?

Analysis and Feeling Questions

4. For those of you who felt bored, can you play the same video game, watch the same movie, do the same job without getting bored? If so, what was the difference here?
5. Even if the activity was not new, what did you learn today that was new?
6. What is the responsibility of the old timers to the people who have never done this before?
7. Did those familiar with the activity assume a leadership role, or did you intentionally not take the lead? What was the rationale for your decision?

Synthesis and Transference Questions

8. In general, what is your responsibility when a leader asks you to do something that you've already done?
9. Did anyone consider asking the leader to do something else because you had done this activity before? If so, what kept you from asking?

Based upon the responses to some of these questions, the facilitator may want to conduct more in-depth discussions about whether:

- Something new is gained the second or third time around.
- Participants need to take greater responsibility for determining the activities that are done.
- It is the leader or the participant who is responsible when boredom sets in.

Notes and Customized Questions

8 Choosing Not to Participate

"The leaders told us that participation was entirely voluntary,
so I decided not to participate."

Fact-Finding Questions

1. All activities here are voluntary. Who chose not to do something today?
2. Did you feel pressure to participate? If so, from where?
3. Was there any pressure not to participate? If so, from where?

Analysis and Feeling Questions

4. Would anyone feel comfortable telling the rest of us why you didn't do the last activity?
5. Now that the activity is over, how do you feel about not participating?
6. Of those who did participate, what do you have to say to those who didn't?
7. What do you think is the purpose of voluntary participation?

Synthesis and Transference Questions

8. To those who did not participate, do you think that you will participate the next time you get a chance? If not, why not? If so, what will make the next time different?
9. To those who did not participate, are you normally cautious? If so, what else have you consciously decided not to do? If not participating was out of the ordinary, why was this time different?
10. Were any of the barriers encountered today also the same barriers that prevent participation in day-to-day activities?

Based upon the responses to some of these questions, the facilitator may want to conduct more in-depth discussions about whether:

- Leaders should sometimes push harder to get people to participate.

- There are some valid reasons not to participate.
- As much learning can occur by observing as by participating.

Notes and Customized Questions

9 Dealing with Frustration

"We were goofing up, people weren't working together, and no one was listening to each other. I was frustrated."

Fact-Finding Questions

1. Is everyone feeling frustrated? By a raise of hands, who is frustrated?
2. By a raise of hands, who noticed that some of you were frustrated?
3. What caused the frustration? Why are you frustrated?
4. When did frustration start?

Analysis and Feeling Questions

5. Did the cause of the frustration begin with this activity, or was it there before? Explain.
6. How did people exhibit their frustration?
7. Was frustration an appropriate response to the events? Why or why not?
8. What effect, either positive or negative, is frustration having on the group?

Synthesis and Transference Questions

9. Is frustration a problem that should be addressed with this group? Why or why not?
10. What specifically can we do to address frustration in the next activity?
11. In general (not specifically the last activity), what frustrates you?
12. Are the things that frustrate you important or trivial? If trivial, why do you let these things bother you?
13. How do you deal with frustration in your daily lives?
14. How can the solutions that we've decided to use in the next activity also be used with your daily frustrations?

Based upon the responses to some of these questions, the facilitator may want to conduct more in-depth discussions about whether:

- Pent-up frustrations lead to more serious problems.
- Trivial frustrations should be addressed or ignored.
- Frustration can be vented in socially acceptable ways.
- People tend to let things bother them needlessly.

Notes and Customized Questions

10 Putting Each Other Down

> "The leaders talked about emotional support within our group, but today some of us put people down."

Fact-Finding Questions

1. What put-downs did you hear during the last activity?
2. What was the specific situation that led to the comments?

Analysis and Feelings Questions

3. What were the intentions of the comments made?
4. What do the people who were put down think about the comments?
5. What do the people who said them think about the comments? Did they consider them put-downs? Be honest. Don't just give an answer that you think will please the leaders.

Synthesis and Transference Questions

6. Are put-downs done in fun sometimes okay? Do they still hurt people? Can they actually enhance teambuilding?
7. Do we need to avoid put-downs in the next activities—or do you think these kinds of put-downs are okay? Explain your answer.
8. If we need to avoid put-downs in the immediate future, give at least one specific thing we can do to avoid them.
9. Do put-downs similar to the ones today occur when you are back at _____(e.g., home, school, work)? If so, describe the situation.
10. What is one thing you can do to minimize destructive put-downs outside of these organized activities?

Based upon the responses to some of these questions, the facilitator may want to conduct more in-depth discussions about whether:

- Put-downs done in fun add or detract from group cohesiveness.

- Put-downs come from the same people all of the time.
- Put-downs are directed at the same people all of the time.
- There are long-term effects of put-downs.

Notes and Customized Questions

11 The Same People Always Leading

*"Every time the leaders give us a task, it is always
the same three people telling the rest of us what to do."*

Fact-Finding Questions

1. By a raise of hands, how many people think that the same few people are always assuming the leadership role?
2. Who are the people assuming leadership?
3. When you say that the same people are always leading, what specifically are they doing?

Analysis and Feeling Questions

4. I am going to put these leaders on the spot a little bit. Why are you doing most of the leading today?
5. Now a question for those who are not leading—why are you taking a follower role today?
6. The facilitators did not assign anyone a leadership role. What led to this arrangement?
7. Both leaders and followers, is this arrangement of leaders and followers okay with everyone? Why or why not?
8. (If it is not okay with everyone) Do you want the facilitators to step in and change the dynamics of the group, or is this something that you want to deal with on your own?
9. (If dealing with it on their own) What steps can the group take to change the leadership?

Synthesis and Transference Questions

10. Describe characteristics that you associate with leadership. What traits do you value in a leader?
11. Several questions back, I asked you to describe what the leaders in this group were actually doing. How does their behavior compare to the traits that you value in a leader?
12. Which leaders most affect your day-to-day lives? How did they get their position of authority? Describe their leadership style. Does it work well for you? Explain.

Based upon the responses to some of these questions, the facilitator may want to conduct more in-depth discussions about:

- Characteristics of an effective leader.
- Characteristics of poor leadership.
- How groups with no assigned leader organize themselves.

Notes and Customized Questions

12 Relating to the Natural World

"My main reason for coming here was not to experience nature, but now I feel a connection with this place."

Fact-Finding Questions

1. Describe the natural surroundings that we were in today.
2. What part of the surroundings most captured your attention?
3. What is one thing about the surroundings that you noticed that others may not have?
4. Did you use any of the four senses other than sight to experience the natural surroundings? If so, which ones?
5. How often do you go to places that you consider natural?
6. Did you do anything today that was disrespectful of this place? If so, what?

Analysis and Feeling Questions

7. What three words best describe your relationship with nature?
8. What happened today that makes you feel closer to the natural world?
9. What is one thing that you will remember about this place?

Synthesis and Transference Questions

10. Do you think that a personal connection with nature is important? Why or why not?
11. What is one thing that you will do that may help protect this place?
12. What is one thing that you do in your daily life that may indirectly harm this place?

Based upon the responses to some of these questions, the facilitator may want to conduct more in-depth discussions about:

- The role that nature plays in our lives.
- Whether one attitude toward nature is better than another.

- What things instill an environmental ethic.

Notes and Customized Questions

13 Having a Vision

> "Now that I see the bigger picture,
> I better understand my role in reaching our goals."

Fact-Finding Questions

1. For a moment, forget about the specifics of the last activity and look at the bigger picture. Why do you think that your group was brought together here today? What are you supposed to get out of today?
2. What happened in the last activity that has anything to do with this bigger purpose?
3. Did you think about the bigger picture while doing the last activity? Why or why not?

Analysis and Feeling Questions

4. To each of you individually, do you think of yourself primarily as a details person or a big-picture, vision-type person? Why do you feel this way?
5. Can a person be both a visionary and a details person, or are people predominantly one or the other? Explain.
6. A vision or detail, which do you value most in a leader? Give specific examples in your own life.

Synthesis and Transference Questions

7. What is the mission of your _____ (e.g., agency, company, team)?
8. If you don't know the mission, why is that?
9. What is your personal mission concerning your affiliation with this _____ (e.g., agency, company, team)?
10. How do you explain the differences between the agency vision and your personal vision? Are the two, from your perspective, compatible?

Based upon the responses to some of these questions, the facilitator may want to conduct more in-depth discussions about whether:

- Visionaries lack a realistic perspective.
- Those without vision lose sight of the things that are really important.
- Society rewards nuts-and-bolts managers over visionaries.
- People often lose the bigger picture in their day-to-day lives.
- Having a vision (personal or group) is important.
- Visions change significantly over time.

Notes and Customized Questions

14 Looking at a Problem in a Whole New Way

"It never occurred to me that we could do it that way."

Fact-Finding Questions

1. How did you solve the last challenge?
2. What led up to the solution? In other words, what did you do that allowed you to find the solution?
3. How was the solution arrived at?
4. Did anyone have doubts about the solution working? What were these doubts?

Analysis and Feeling Questions

5. What barriers were overcome to arrive at the solution? Be specific.
6. Who would not have thought of the solution on their own? Why not?
7. In retrospect, what could have been done to make the solution even better?

Synthesis and Transference Questions

8. Of the barriers mentioned, do any of them carry over to everyday life?
9. Give one example of a limitation (obstacle) that you deal with on a regular basis.
10. How do you cope with that limitation?
11. Does anyone have suggestions for another way to deal with that limitation?
12. In looking at the solution to this problem, is there anything that you did here that we need to carry over to other activities that we do?

Based upon the responses to some of these questions, the facilitator may want to conduct more in-depth discussions about whether:

- All of us carry assumptions that get in the way of creative thinking.

- Some assumptions about limitations are accurate and need to be accepted.
- Creative thinking is a natural or a learned skill.
- Habit interferes with original thinking.

Notes and Customized Questions

15 Not Completing the Task

> "We had a challenge and a goal,
> but stopped before completing the challenge."

Fact-Finding Questions

1. What was the objective of this last activity?
2. Was it accomplished to your satisfaction? If so, what exactly were you trying to accomplish? If not, what specifically did not get accomplished?
3. What are three factors that prevented you from completing the task?

Analysis and Feeling Questions

4. Would you call what just happened "a failure?" Why or why not?
5. Explain your feelings about not finishing.
6. Were you ready for this task? Explain.
7. Was it too difficult? Explain.

Synthesis and Transference Questions

8. While the objective of the last activity may have been to complete a specific task, what is the primary goal of the entire program?
9. Concerning the overriding goal of the program, was this last activity a failure? Why or why not?
10. Is it possible to actually complete an assigned task, but still fail? Explain.
11. Is it possible to not complete a task, but consider the effort worthwhile? Explain.
12. If you had to do the task over again, what would you do differently?
13. What is one thing in every day life that you have left unfinished?

Based upon the responses to some of these questions, the facilitator may want to conduct more in-depth discussions about whether:

- Failure is a good or a bad thing.
- The failure was as individuals or as a group.
- Excessive attention to the task jeopardizes group dynamics (relationships).

Notes and Customized Questions

16 Complacent About Safety

"This time we did not look out for each other's safety
as much as we should have."

Fact-Finding Questions

1. What were the potential risks of the last activity? When during the activity could someone have gotten hurt?
2. Specifically, what just happened that was not safe?
3. Was the problem with safety due to the activity or to the way in which the group did the activity?

Analysis and Feeling Questions

4. What is the main reason that the lapse in safety happened?
5. Can you think of anything today that is more important than having a safe experience? If so, what? If not, why is safety the most important thing?
6. Are the safety rules overly cautious? Why or why not?

Synthesis and Transference Questions

7. What can the participants do to avoid lapses in safety?
8. Is there anything that the facilitators should do to keep this from reoccurring?
9. Do you think that this group is ready for activities that have potential physical risk? Why or why not?
10. Should there be individuals specifically assigned to safety considerations? What are the pros and cons of this?

Based upon the responses to some of these questions, the facilitator may want to conduct more in-depth discussions about whether:

- Boredom leads to complacency.
- When participants feel that safety requirements for some activities are overly strict, there is a tendency to underestimate the potential risk.

Notes and Customized Questions

17 Not Following the Rules

"We completed the activity, but we didn't follow the rules exactly."

Fact-Finding Questions

1. Specifically, what did you do to cut corners on the rules?
2. When did you realize the infraction? How did you react?
3. Do you think the leader realized the infractions?

Analysis and Feeling Questions

4. Would it be fair to call your actions cheating? Why or why not?
5. Why did you not follow the rules?
6. Was it okay, in this situation, to cheat a little bit? Why or why not?
7. What do you think the leaders thought about the infractions?
8. What should leaders do when they notice infractions of the rules?

Synthesis and Transference Questions

9. In terms of breaking the rules, how is this activity different from other activities in life? In other words, do you stretch the rules in everyday life? If so, give examples.
10. I am wondering how you draw the line on breaking rules. What is one specific example of when it is okay and one when it is not?
11. I think some participants were waiting for the leaders to catch you and make you obey the rules. Why were people waiting for the leaders to act?
12. Why does getting caught at breaking the rules by the leaders make the difference?
13. If the leader saw you break the rules, why do you suppose he/she let it slide?
14. Should we do anything different about breaking rules in the next activity? If so, what?

Based upon the responses to some of these questions, the facilitator may want to conduct more in-depth discussions about whether:

- The end justifies the means.
- Boredom with an activity merits cheating or making a less quality effort.
- Doing something the easy and quick way is appropriate.
- Calling someone else on their rule breaking is "snitching."

Notes and Customized Questions

18 Each Person Making A Unique Contribution

"Each of us is important to the group;
each has a slightly different role."

Fact-Finding Questions

1. Going around the circle, I'd like each person to identify a specific contribution you made to the group in the last activity.
2. Is this a role you usually take, or is this something different? Explain.
3. Did any of you assume roles that detracted from the success of the group? If so, what did you do?

Analysis and Feeling Questions

4. For this group, what was the most important objective during this activity?
5. Based on what is the most important objective, what were the key roles that people assumed?
6. Were all of the strengths of the group utilized? If not, why not?

Synthesis and Transference Questions

7. Some of you assumed leadership roles. Are the people who assumed leadership for this activity the same people who usually lead?
8. Some people made sure that everyone was involved and felt part of the group. Are the people who served this role the same people who usually do this? Explain.
9. If people assumed their usual roles, is that the way all of you prefer it? Why or why not?
10. If people did not assume their usual roles, how was today different from _____(e.g., home, school, work)? Is this change a good thing? Explain.

Based upon the responses to some of these questions, the facilitator may want to conduct more in-depth discussions about whether:

- Some people always take over the leadership role.
- Some people always make sure everyone is involved.
- Some people always sit back and do not fully participate.
- Some people care only about goals, not about the people involved (and others care about people, but not the goals).

Notes and Customized Questions

19 Trusting

> "There is trusting someone during a specific activity,
> and there is ongoing genuine trust.
> They are two different things."

Fact-Finding Questions

1. What were the exact moments during the last activity where trust was needed?
2. How did the people who were trusted handle that trust?

Analysis and Feeling Questions

3. What are three specific things that a person can do to build trust?
4. What are three specific things that a person can do to break down trust?
5. Have you personally done any of those things that break down trust? If so, why did you do them?

Synthesis and Transference Questions

6. How was trust for this activity any different from the trust that occurs on a day-to-day basis?
7. How would you describe the level of trust at _____(e.g., home, school, work, the institution)?
8. How does that level of trust affect your feeling about _____ _____(e.g., school, work, home, the institution)?
9. What is your role in creating that level of trust? Specifically how do you build trust? How do you break it down?
10. Did we enhance or damage trust during the last activity? Explain.

Based upon the responses to some of these questions, the facilitator may want to conduct more in-depth discussions about whether:

- Trust is the primary factor in the happiness or misery at a particular time and/or place.
- Distrust curtails progress and cooperation.

- Distrust of bosses or teachers or counselors is well-founded.
- People you don't trust do not trust you.
- Trusting and trustworthiness are related.

Notes and Customized Questions

20 Working as a Team

"I really think that the success of the last activity
was because we worked together as a team."

Fact-Finding Questions

1. Provide two specific instances of the group exhibiting team-work.
2. Provide one specific example of where the teamwork broke down.
3. By a raise of hands, how many people were satisfied with the level of teamwork in this activity? How many were not?

Analysis and Feeling Questions

4. (Based on Q3) Give one reason why you were not satisfied with the level of teamwork. Give one reason why you were satisfied.
5. In my opinion, teamwork means everyone feels free to express their ideas. Did anyone have an idea, but not express it? If so, explain why it was withheld?
6. In my opinion, teamwork also means that all expressed ideas are acknowledged, even if they are not used. Did anyone feel that your ideas were not listened to? If so, explain the situation.

Synthesis and Transference Questions

7. What is one thing we can do in the next activity to ensure teamwork and avoid the problems that occurred this time?
8. Are there examples of teamwork that you saw here that remind you of _____ (e.g., home, school, work)? If not, what is the difference between here and there?
9. Are the problems of teamwork exhibited here the same problems as at _____ (e.g., home, school, work)? If so, what are they?
10. Pick one problem in teamwork that occurred here that also is a problem at _____ (e.g., home, school, work)— and make one solid suggestion for addressing the problem.

Based upon the responses to some of these questions, the facilitator may want to conduct more in-depth discussions about whether:

- Lack of teamwork centers on personal conflicts between two individuals or two groups of individuals (cliques).
- Friendly competition contributes to or detracts from teamwork.

Notes and Customized Questions

21 A Final Processing Session

> "I've really enjoyed our time together.
> Before we part ways, I'd like to have one final discussion."

The last processing session before the end of an educational program is unique. A sense of closure, which may not have been a concern before, now takes precedence. The following is a short list of questions that may be useful for the final processing session:

Fact-Finding Questions

1. In no more than two sentences, summarize the key events of the _____ (day, week, etc.).
2. Five years from now, what is the one thing that you will remember about the program? Why will that thing stand out?
3. In which area did you see progress? Explain.

Analysis and Feeling Questions

4. After participating in all of the things that we did together, what is one thing that you learned about yourself? (This question can be open-ended, or it can be more specific, e.g., identify a hidden strength or a revealed weakness.)
5. Thinking in terms of the group as a whole, what was the most important thing that happened during the program? Why was it important?
6. Thinking in terms of you as an individual, what was the most important thing that happened during the program? Why was it important?
7. What connections are there between the most important group things that you identified and the most important individual things?

Synthesis and Transference Questions

8. Throughout the program, we have talked about changes that each of us can make. I now want each of you to make a verbal commitment. What is one thing back at _____ (e.g., work, school) that you promise to do because of all

that you learned and accomplished here?

9. What exactly do you promise to carry forward that will give this program purpose?

Based upon the responses to some of these questions, the facilitator may want to conduct more in-depth discussions about:

- Reasons for actively seeking out educational experiences.
- The important of explicitly identifying the lessons of experience.
- Whether the final processing session should highlight the positive, as opposed to the negative, aspects of the experience.

Notes and Customized Questions

Notes

PREFACE

[1] Knapp, C. E. 1992. *Lasting Lessons: A Teacher's Guide to Reflecting on Experience.* Charleston, WV: ERIC/Clearinghouse on Rural Education and Small Schools. Also Nadler, R. S., & Luckner, J. L. 1992. *Processing the Adventure Experience: Theory and Practice.* Dubuque: Kendall/Hunt.

CHAPTER 2

[1] Luckner, J. L., & Nadler, R. S. 1997. *Processing the Experience: Strategies to Enhance and Generalize Learning (2nd ed).* Dubuque: Kendall/Hunt, p. 8.
[2] Sugerman, D. A., Doherty, K. L., Garvey, D. E., & Gass, M. A. 2000. *Reflective Learning: Theory and Practice.* Dubuque: Kendall/Hunt, p. 1.
[3] Joplin, L. 1981. On Defining Experiential Education. *Journal of Experiential Education,* 4(1): 17-20.
[4] Ni, H. C. 1997. *Entering the Tao: Master Ni's Guidance for Self-Cultivation.* Boston: Shambhala, p. 17.
[5] Knapp, C. E. 1992. *Lasting Lessons: A Teacher's Guide to Reflecting on Experience.* Charleston, WV: ERIC/Clearinghouse on Rural Education and Small Schools, p. 15.
[6] Hammel, H. 1986. How to design a debriefing session. *Journal of Experiential Education,* 9(3): 20-25.

CHAPTER 3

[1] Pearson, M., & Smith, D. 1985. "Debriefing in Experience-Based Learning." In D. Boud, R. Keogh, & D. Walker, eds., *Reflection: Turning Experience into Learning.* London: Nichols Publishing.
[2] Merton, T. 1955. *No Man is an Island.* San Diego: Harcourt Brace Hovanovich, p. 124.
[3] The session was "Three Steps to Better Processing," by Steve Simpson & Dan Miller, presented at the Annual Association for Experiential Education Conference, Vancouver, BC, November 2003.

CHAPTER 5

[1] Simpson, S., Miller, D., & Bocher, B. 1998. Chiji Processing Cards and Non-directive Facilitated Processing. In *Association for Experiential Education 25th Annual International Conference Proceedings.* Boulder, CO: Association for Experiential Education, pp. 261-271.
[2] Bacon, S. 1987. *The Evolution of the Outward Bound Process.* Greenwich, CT: Outward Bound (ERIC Document Reproduction Service No.

ED 295 780. Also on-line at http://www.wilderdom.com/html/Bacon1987EvolutionOBProcess.html

³ James, T. 1980. *Can the Mountains Speak for Themselves?* On-line at http://www.wilderdom.com/facilitation/Mountains.html

⁴ In addition to descriptions in Bacon's *The Evolution of the Outward Bound Process*, Outward Bound Plus, the Metaphoric Curriculum Model, and Mountains Speak for Themselves are summarized well in Michael Gass's "The Evolution of Processing Adventure Therapy Experiences," a chapter in Gass, M.A., ed. 1993. *Adventure Therapy: Therapeutic Applications of Adventure Programming.* Dubuque, IA: Kendall/Hunt.

⁵ A continuum with four categories, of course, is only one way to delineate processing styles or techniques. Priest and Gass, for example, divide facilitation (including processing) into six distinct generations. The main difference between their delineation and ours is they look at metaphors and frontloading in much greater detail, an approach that is most applicable to therapeutic programs. Priest, S., and Gass, M. A. 1997. *Effective Leadership in Adventure Programming.* Champaign, IL: Human Kinetics. In a different publication, Priest and Gass, this time with Lee Gillis, suggest that processing can be looked at, not so much as facilitator-centered/participant-centered, but as problem-focused/solution-focused. Priest, Gass, and Gillis point out that facilitators sometimes want to emphasize a group's strengths and at other times want to address a group's weaknesses. Processing about strengths will differ from processing about weaknesses. Priest, S., Gass, M., & Gillis, L. 2000. *The Essential Elements of Facilitation.* Dubuque, IA: Kendall/Hunt.

⁶ Hershey, P. 1984. *The Situational Leader.* New York: Warner Books.

CHAPTER 6

¹ The session titled "The Processing Methodology Spectrum and Therapeutic Recreation" was presented at the Midwest Symposium on Therapeutic Recreation, Springfield, IL, April 1998.

² This is an often quoted Hindu Proverb. One online source is Inspiration Peak at http://www.inspirationpeak.com/cgi-bin/search.cgi?keyword=teach

CHAPTER 7

¹ Bacon, S. 1983. *The Conscious Use of Metaphor in Outward Bound.* Denver: Colorado Outward Bound School, p. 23-49.

² The Leopold Education Project (LEP) has developed environmental education programs designed around the Land Ethic and Leopold's classic book, *A Sand County Almanac.* LEP has a Web site at http://www.lep.org

³ Eiseley, L. 1946. *The Immense Journey.* New York: Vintage Books. p. 18-20.

CHAPTER 8

[1] Knapp, C. E. 1992. *Lasting Lessons: A Teacher's Guide to Reflecting on Experience*. Charleston, WV: ERIC/Clearinghous on Rural Education and Small Schools, p. 68.

[2] Luckner, J. L., & Nadler, R. S. 1997. *Processing the Experience: Strategies to Enhance and Generalize Learning (2nd ed)*. Dubuque, IA: Kendall/Hunt, pp. 31-34.

[3] Quinsland, L. K., & Van Ginkel, A. 1984. How to Process Experience. *Journal of Experiential Education*, 7(2), 8-13.

[4] Knapp, 1992, pp. 62-65.

CHAPTER 9

[1] Lao Tzu. 1989. *Tao Te Ching*, John C. H. Chu, trans. Boston: Shambhala, Chapter 17.

[2] Dewey, J. 1938. *Experience and Education*. New York: Simon and Schuster, p. 27.

[3] Simpson, S. 2003. *The Leader Who is Hardly Known: Self-less Teaching from the Chinese Tradition*. Oklahoma City: Wood 'N' Barnes, pp. 5-6.

[4] Educators, among them John Dewey and Krishnamurti, elaborate on the importance of this second step. Dewey, J. 1938. *Experience and Education*. New York: Simon and Schuster, pp. 18-19. Krishnamurti, J. 1953. *Education and the Significance of Life*. San Francisco: Harper San Francisco, p. 10.

CHAPTER 10

[1] Bacon, S. 1987. *The Evolution of the Outward Bound Process*. Greenwich, CT: Outward Bound (ERIC Document Reproduction Service No. ED 295 780. Also on-line at http://www.wilderdom.com/html/Bacon1987EvolutionOBProcess.html. Also James, T. 1980. *Can the Mountains Speak for Themselves?* Online at http://www.wilderdom.com/facilitation/Mountains.html

[2] Sax, J. 1980. *Mountains Without Handrails*. Ann Arbor: University of Michigan Press, p. 43.

[3] Knapp, C. 2005. "The Mountains Can't Always Speak for Themselves." In Knapp, C., & Smith, T. eds. *Exploring the Power of Solo, Silence, and Solitude*. Boulder, CO: Association for Experiential Education, p. 20.

APPENDIX A

[1] Sugerman, D., Doherty, K., Garvey, D., & Gass, M. 2000. *Reflective Learning: Theory and Practice*. Dubuque, IA: Kendall/Hunt.

[2] Cain, J., Cummings, M., & Stanchfield, J. 2005. *A Teachable Moment: A Facilitator's Guide to Activities for Processing, Debriefing, Reviewing and Reflection*. Dubuque, IA: Kendall/Hunt.

[1] Knapp, C. 1992. *Lasting Lessons: A Teacher's Guide to Reflecting on Experience.* Charleston, WV: ERIC Clearinghouse on Rural Education and Small Schools.

[2] Luckner, J. L., & Nadler, R. S. 1997. *Processing the Experience: Strategies to Enhance and Generalize Learning (2nd ed).* Dubuque, IA: Kendall/Hunt.

[3] Quinsland, L., & Van Ginkel, A. 1984. How to Process Experience. *Journal of Experiential Education,* 7(2), 8-13.

About the Authors

STEVEN SIMPSON, PhD, is professor of Recreation Management and Therapeutic Recreation at the University of Wisconsin-La-Crosse. He is the former editor of the *Journal of Experiential Education* and has written over 50 articles on experiential education, outdoor recreation, and environmental ethics. Steve can be contacted by e-mail at simpson.stev@uwlax.edu

DAN MILLER is vice president of the Institute for Experiential Education, a former ropes course builder/trainer for ABEE, and a senior instructor for Training Master International Limited in Hong Kong. He has worked in therapeutic recreation for the Family and Children Center and Mayo Clinic.

BUZZ BOCHER is president of the Institute for Experiential Education and, with Dan Miller, the co-creator of Chiji Processing Cards. He is the instructor of environmental studies at the University of Wisconsin-La Crosse and the former director of the university's ropes and challenge course. Buzz can be contacted by e-mail at bocher.wayn@uwlax.edu